TABLE OF CONTENTS

ISBN: 978-1-936058-01-3

DEFINITIONS OF WELDING TERMS

AC or Alternating Current: Is that kind of electricity which reverses its direction periodically. For 60 cycle current, the current goes in one direction and then in the other direction 60 times in the same second, so that the current changes its direction 120 times in one second.

Arc Blow: The deflection of an arc from its normal path because of magnetic forces.

Arc Length: The distance from the tip of the welding electrode to the adjacent surface of the weld pool.

Arc Voltage: The voltage across the welding arc.

As-Welded: Pertaining to the condition of weld metal, welded joints, and weldments after welding, but prior to any subsequent thermal, mechanical, or chemical treatments.

Autogenous Weld: A fusion weld made without filler metal.

Backing: A material or device placed against the back side of the joint, or at both sides of a weld in electroslag and electrogas welding, to support and retain molten weld metal. The material may be partially fused or remain unfused during welding and may be either metal or nonmetal.

Backstep Sequence: A longitudinal sequence in which weld passes are made in the direction opposite to the progress of welding.

Bare Electrode: A filler metal electrode that has been produced as a wire, strip, or bar with no coating or covering other than that incidental to its manufacture or preservation.

Base Metal: The metal or alloy that is welded, brazed, soldered, or cut.

Butt Weld: A nonstandard term for a weld in a butt joint..

Covered Electrode: A composite filler metal electrode consisting of a core of a bare electrode or metal cored electrode to which a covering sufficient to provide a slag layer on the weld metal has been applied. The covering may contain materials providing such functions as shielding from the atmosphere, deoxidation, and arc stabilization, and can serve as a source of metallic additions to the weld.

Crater: A depression in the weld face at the termination of a weld bead.

Depth of Fusion: The distance that fusion extends into the base metal or previous bead from the surface melted during welding.

DC or Direct Current: Electrode current which flows only in one direction. In welding an arc welding process wherein the power supply at the arc is direct current.

Electrode Angles: Electrode angles help to control the shape of the puddle and the amount of penetration. The *work angle* is the angle between the electrode and the work surface along the work plane which runs perpendicular to the axis of the weld.

The *travel angle* is the angle between the joint and the electrode along the axis of the weld. A *push* angle exists when the electrode points in the direction of the travel. A *drag* angle points away from the direction of travel.

Compared to a clock face, 1 minute of time equals approximately 6° of electrode angle.

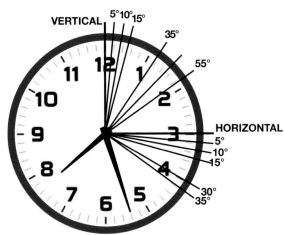

Fillet Weld: A weld of approximately triangular cross section joining two surfaces approximately at right angles to each other in a lap joint, T-joint, or corner joint.

Fillet Weld Leg: The distance from the joint root to the toe of the fillet weld.

Flat Welding Position: The welding position used to weld from the upper side of the joint at a point where the weld axis is approximately horizontal, and the weld face lies in an approximately horizontal plane.

Flux: A material used to hinder or prevent the formation of oxides and other undesirable substances in molten metal and on solid metal surfaces, and to dissolve or otherwise facilitate the removal of such substances.

Gas Pocket: A nonstandard term for porosity.

Gas Shielded Arc Welding: A group of processes including electrogas welding, flux cored arc welding, gas metal arc welding, gas tungsten arc welding, and plasma arc welding.

Groove Weld: A weld made in a groove between the workpieces.

Heat Affected Zone: The portion of the base metal whose mechanical properties or microstructure have been altered by the heat of welding, brazing, soldering, or thermal cutting.

High Carbon Steel: Steel containing .45% carbon or more.

Horizontal Welding Position, *fillet weld*: The welding position in which the weld is on the upper side of an approximately horizontal surface and against an approximately vertical surface.

Horizontal Welding Position, *groove weld*: The welding position in which the weld face lies in an approximately vertical plane and the weld axis at the point of welding is approximately horizontal.

Lap Joint: A joint between two overlapping members in parallel planes.

Low Carbon Steel: Steel containing .20% or less carbon. Also mild steel.

Melting Rate: The weight or length of electrode, wire, rod, powder melted in a unit of time.

Mig Welding: A nonstandard term for gas metal arc welding and flux cored arc welding.

Molten Weld Pool: A nonstandard term for weld pool.

Open-Circuit Voltage: The voltage between the output terminals of the power source when no current is flowing to the torch or gun.

Overhead Welding Position: The welding position in which welding is performed from the underside of the joint.

Overlap: A nonstandard term when used for incomplete fusion.

Penetration: A nonstandard term when used for depth of fusion, joint penetration, or root penetration.

Porosity: Cavity-type discontinuities formed by gas entrapment during solidification or in a thermal spray deposit.

Postheating: The application of heat to an assembly after welding, brazing, soldering, thermal spraying, or thermal cutting.

Preheat: The heat applied to the base metal or substrate to attain and maintain preheat temperature.

Radiography: The use of radiant energy in the form of X-rays or gamma rays for the nondestructive examination of metals.

Reverse Polarity: A nonstandard term for direct current electrode positive.

Root Opening: A separation at the joint root between the workpieces.

Shielded Metal Arc Welding (SMAW): An arc welding process with an arc between a covered electrode and the weld pool. The process is used with shielding from the decomposition of the electrode covering, without the application of pressure, and with filler metal from the electrode.

Slag Inclusion: Non-metallic solid material entrapped in weld metal or between weld metal and base metal.

Spatter: The metal particles expelled during fusion welding that do not form a part of the weld.

Straight Polarity: A nonstandard term for direct current electrode negative.

Stress-Relief Heat Treatment: Uniform heating of a structure or a portion thereof to a sufficient temperature to relieve the major portion of the residual stresses, followed by uniform cooling.

String Bead: A type of weld bead made without appreciable transverse oscillation.

Stringer Bead: A type of weld bead made without appreciable weaving motion.

Tack Weld: A weld made to hold the parts of a weldment in proper alignment until the final welds are made.

Throat of a Fillet Weld-

    • **Theoretical Throat:** The distance from the beginning of the joint root perpendicular to the hypotenuse of the largest right triangle that can be inscribed within the cross section of a fillet weld. This dimension is based on the assumption that the root opening is equal to zero.

    • **Actual Throat:** The shortest distance between the weld root and the face of a fillet.

    • **Effective Throat:** The minimum distance minus any convexity between the weld root and the face fo a fillet weld.

Thoriated Tungsten: Tungsten containing a small percentage of thorium. The electronic emission quality of the electrode is improved.

TIG Welding: A nonstandard term for gas tungsten arc welding.

Ultimate Tensile Strength: The maximum tensile strength which will cause a material to break (usually expressed in pounds per square inch).

Underbead Crack: A crack in the heat-affected zone generally not extending to the surface of the base metal.

Undercut: A groove melted into the base metal adjacent to the weld toe or weld root and left unfilled by weld metal.

Uphill Welding: A pipe welding term indicating that the welds are made from the bottom of the pipe to the top of the pipe. The pipe is not rotated.

Vertical Welding Position: The welding position in which the weld axis, at the point of welding, is approximately vertical, and the weld face lies in an approximately vertical plane.

Weave Bead: A type of weld bead made with transverse oscillation.

Weld: A localized coalescence of metals or nonmetals produced either by heating the materials to the welding temperature, with or without the application of pressure, or by the application of pressure alone and with or without the use of filler materials.

Weld Face: The exposed surface of a weld on the side from which welding was done.

Weld Metal: The portion of a fusion weld that has been completely melted during welding.

Weld Pass: A single progression of welding along a joint. The result of a pass is a weld bead or layer.

Weld Root: The points, shown in a cross section, at which the root surface intersects the base metal surfaces.

Weld Toe: The junction of the weld face and the base metal.**Weldment:** An assembly whose component parts are joined by welding.

Welding Procedure: The detailed methods and practices involved in the production of a weldment.

Welding Position: The relationship between the weld pool, joint, joint members, and welding heat source during welding.

Welding Rod: A form of welding filler metal, normally packaged in straight lengths, that does not conduct the welding current.

Whipping: A manual welding technique in which the arc or flame is manipulated to alternate backwards and forwards as it progresses along the weld path.

WELDING TEST POSITIONS

Fillet Welds

FLAT POSITION 1F	HORIZONTAL POSITION 2F	VERTICAL POSITION 3F	OVERHEAD POSITION 4F
Axis of Weld Horizontal	Axis of Weld Horizontal	Axis of Weld Vertical	Axis of Weld Horizontal

Groove Welds

FLAT POSITION 1G	HORIZONTAL POSITION 2G	VERTICAL POSITION 3G	OVERHEAD POSITION 4G
Plates, Axis of Weld Horizontal	Plates vertical, Axis of Weld Horizontal	Plates vertical, Axis of Weld Vertical	Plates Overhead, Axis of Weld Horizontal

FLAT 1G	HORIZONTAL 2G	HORIZONTAL FIXED 5G	45° FIXED 6G
		"Bell Hole"	"Arkansas Bell Hole" 45° ±5°
Pipe *shall be turned or rolled* while welding axis of pipe horizontal	Axis of Pipe Vertical	Pipe *shall not be turned or rolled* while welding axis of pipe horizontal	Pipe stationary with axis approximately 45°

WELD NOMENCLATURE

B – Butt	C – Corner	E – Edge	L – Lap	T – Tee

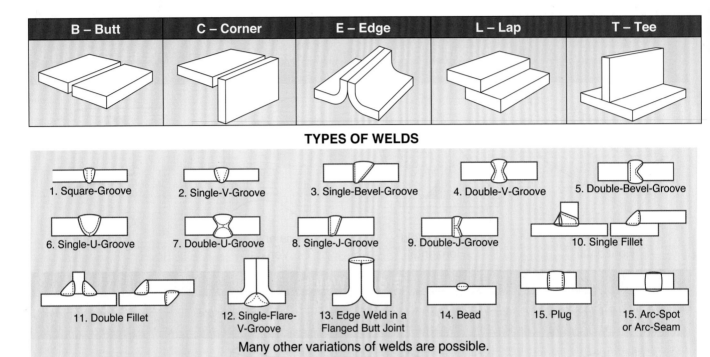

TYPES OF WELDS

1. Square-Groove
2. Single-V-Groove
3. Single-Bevel-Groove
4. Double-V-Groove
5. Double-Bevel-Groove
6. Single-U-Groove
7. Double-U-Groove
8. Single-J-Groove
9. Double-J-Groove
10. Single Fillet
11. Double Fillet
12. Single-Flare-V-Groove
13. Edge Weld in a Flanged Butt Joint
14. Bead
15. Plug
15. Arc-Spot or Arc-Seam

Many other variations of welds are possible.

WELD NOMENCLATURE

Groove Weld	Fillet Weld

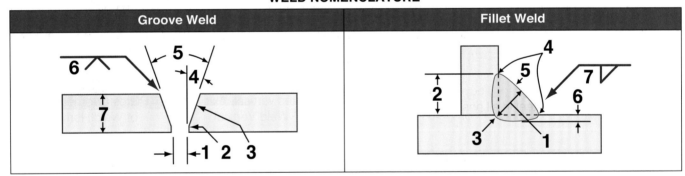

1. **ROOT OPENING (RO):** the separation between the members to be joined at the root of the joint.

2. **ROOT FACE (RF):** Groove face adjacent to the root of the joint.

3. **GROOVE FACE:** The surface of a member included in the groove.

4. **BEVEL ANGLE (A):** the angle formed between the prepared edge of a member and a plane perpendicular to the surface of the member.

5. **GROOVE ANGLE (A):** the total included angle of the groove between parts to be joined by a groove weld.

6. **SIZE OF WELD (S):** the joint penetration (depth of bevel plus the root penetration when specified). The size of a groove weld and its effective throat are one in the same.

7. **PLATE THICKNESS (T):** Thickness of plate welded.

1. **ACTUAL THROAT OF A FILLET WELD:** The shortest distance from the root of the fillet weld to its face.

2. **LEG OF A FILLET WELD:** The distance from the root of the joint to the toe of the fillet weld.

3. **ROOT OF A WELD:** The points at which the back of the weld intersects the base metal surfaces.

4. **TOE OF A WELD:** The junction between the face of the weld and the base metal.

5. **FACE OF WELD:** The exposed surface of a weld on the side from which the welding was done.

6. **DEPTH OF FUSION:** The distance that fusion extends into the base metal or previous pass from the surface melted during welding.

7. **SIZE OF WELD (S):** Leg length of the fillet.

SHIELDED METAL ARC WELDING - STRUCTURAL COURSE OVERVIEW

Objective: **The objective of this course is to provide you with advanced skills in shielded metal arc welding.**

The Shielded Metal Arc Welding - Structural course is designed to provide the student with:

- A thorough understanding of the safety precautions for shielded metal arc welding, and an awareness of the importance of safety in welding;

- An advanced understanding of the shielded metal arc process and equipment along with the key variables that affect the quality of welds (electrode selection, polarity and amperage, arc length, travel speed and electrode angles);

- The role of the welder in visual inspection and quality control;

- Welding related information included on weld size and profile, carbon arc cutting and gouging, hard-surfacing, the repair of cast iron and metals identification.

- Video demonstrations and skill building exercises involving:

  - Multi-pass single v-groove welds on 3/8" and 1" mild steel in all positions;

  - Standard Horizontal (2G) and Vertical (3G) qualification tests on 3/8" mild steel as a specified standard for entry level welders.

Prerequisites

The student should have successfully completed the Hobart Institute of Welding Technology's Shielded Metal Arc Welding - Basic course or have the equivalent experience.

The student must be able to pass a 1/4" fillet weld break test in the horizontal position and overhead positions (Topics 11 and 24 in SMAWB), a square groove guided bend test in the horizontal position (Topic 14 in SMAWB) and a square groove guided bend test in the vertical up position (Topic 20 in SMAWB.)

Testing

To pass the Shielded Metal Arc Welding Structural course, the student is required to pass:

- Written tests on the shielded metal arc welding process;

- Visual inspection and standard guided bend tests in the horizontal, vertical up and overhead positions on 3/8" mild steel plate.

- Visual inspection and standard guided bend tests in the horizontal, vertical up, overhead and flat positions on 1" mild steel block.

Safety Equipment & Tools

You will need the following safety equipment and tools for the exercises in this course:

- Nonflammable welding jacket or welding leathers;

- Safety glasses with side shields;

- Welding helmet with proper lens shades based on welding amperage;

- Steel-toed safety boots;

- Denim pants without cuffs;

- 1 pair of heavy duty leather gloves;

- 1 pair of pliers for handling hot parts;

- 1 wire brush;

- 1 chipping hammer.

INTRODUCTION TO SHIELDED METAL ARC WELDING

Objective: **To give you a better understanding of the shielded metal arc welding applications and advantages in the workplace.**

Introduction

The shielded metal arc welding process is a metal joining process that fuses parts together by heat from an electric arc between a consumable flux-coated electrode and the work... Shielding is provided by a breakdown of the flux coating.

Historical and General Information

Growth of this process was slow until 1930, when it was recognized as a major metal joining method. It is still widely used today, although automated welding processes have replaced shielded metal arc in many applications.

Shielded metal arc welding is almost always used in manual applications. It is not very adaptable to semi-automatic, mechanized, or automatic applications.

Shielded Metal Arc Welding (SMAW) is most commonly used to weld ferrous metals such as: low carbon and alloy steels, quenched and tempered steel. It can also be used to weld stainless steel, and cast iron, however nonferrous metals are not as easily welded with shielded metal arc.

Copper and copper alloys, nickel and nickel alloys, and even aluminum and aluminum alloys are weldable on occasion.

Advantages & Disadvantages of SMAW

As mentioned earlier, shielded metal arc welding is one of the most popular welding processes. There are several reasons for this.

Advantages of SMAW

- Auxiliary shielding gas not required.
- Can weld from a remote power source
- Less sensitive to wind

The flux coating on the electrode breaks down to form shielding gas, so auxiliary shielding is not required as it is with gas metal arc and gas tungsten arc welding.

Structural welding is the welding of buildings and bridges. The shielded metal arc process is used in structural steel erection because of the simplicity of equipment.

Shielded metal arc is also used to weld all sorts of pipe, in many different sizes and wall thicknesses.

Portability is an important factor, since many times the power source must be located a considerable distance from the welding job. With shielded metal arc welding only the electrode holder and work lead need to be carried to the work.

Another advantage of shielded metal arc is its capability to weld thin to thick materials in a variety of tensile strengths, due to the wide range of electrode diameters and types available.

And because SMAW is versatile, it is an all position process used for field welding of storage tanks, pressure vessels, industrial piping, transmission pipeline, and steel structures.

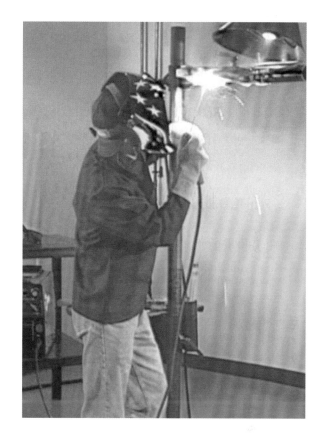

Disadvantages of SMAW

- More labor intensive and has a lower productivity rate

- 60% to 65% process efficiency rating

- Amperage is restricted by the electrode.

SMAW is more labor intensive, and productivity rates are lower than with continuous wire processes like gas metal arc welding and flux cored arc welding, because the welder has to stop to change electrodes and chip slag.

SMAW has a process efficiency rating of about 60 to 65 percent, which means that 35 to 40 percent of electrodes end up as waste due to stub loss, slag production and shielding gas formation.

Also, amperage is restricted to the current carrying capability of the electrode.

To summarize, shielded metal arc welding is the most widely used of the various welding processes because of its versatility and portability.

SAFETY & HEALTH OF WELDERS

Objective: **To become familiar with the important safety rules associated with all phases of welding.**

Summary of Safety Precautions for Arc Welding

1. Make sure your arc welding equipment is installed correctly, properly grounded, and in good working condition.

2. Always wear protective clothing suitable for the welding to be done.

3. Always wear proper eye protection when welding, grinding or cutting.

4. Keep your work area clean and free of hazards. Make sure that no flammable, volatile or explosive materials are in or near the work area.

5. Handle all compressed gas cylinders with extreme care. Keep caps on when not in use.

6. Make sure that compressed gas cylinders are secured to the wall or to other structural supports.

7. When a compressed gas cylinder is empty, close the valve and mark the cylinder "EMPTY."

8. Do not weld in a confined space without taking special precautions.

9. Do not weld on containers that have held combustibles without taking special precautions.

10. Do not weld on sealed containers or compartments without providing vents and taking special precautions.

11. Use mechanical exhaust at the point of welding when welding lead, cadmium, chromium, manganese, brass, bronze, zinc or galvanized steel.

12. Wear rubber boots and stand on a dry insulated platform when welding in a damp or wet area.

13. If it is necessary to splice lengths of welding cable together, make sure all electrical connections are tight and insulated. Do not use cables with frayed, cracked or bare spots in the insulation.

14. When the electrode holder is not in use, hang it on brackets provided. Never let it touch a compressed gas cylinder.

15. Wire stubs on the floor are safety hazards. Therefore, dispose of electrode stubs in proper containers.

16. Shield others from the light rays produced by your welding arc.

17. Do not weld near degreasing operations.

18. When working above ground make sure that scaffold, ladder or work surface is solid and properly secured.

19. Use a safety belt or lifeline when welding in high places without railings.

20. When using water-cooled equipment, check for water leakage.

21. Read and understand all applicable Safety Data Sheets (SDS) that may be used in any welding application.

22. Notify Supervisor of any problems or potential hazards. Follow Lockout/Tagout procedure.

References

For a complete discussion of safety in welding, refer to the following resources:

- The "Welding Safety" section of the Shielded Metal Arc Welding Technical Guide (EW472).

- The American National Standard Z49.1, "Safety In Welding and Cutting", published by the American Welding Society, 8669 NW 36th St., Miami, Florida, 33166.

- "OSHA Safety and Health Standards", 29 CFR 1910, available from the U.S. Department of Labor, Washington, D.C. 20210.

- "Safety and Health of Welders" (EW607), from the Hobart Institute of Welding Technology.

- The "Safety and Health of Welders" video (DV91.0), from the Hobart Institute of Welding Technology.

Objective: To produce quality multi-pass single v-groove welds in the horizontal…or 2G position with a backing strip.

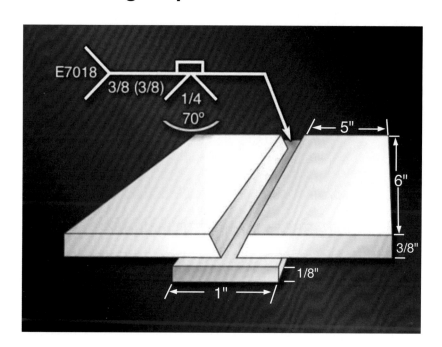

1. Materials & Machine Settings

Base Metal: 3/8" (9.5mm) x 5" (127mm) x 6" (152mm) mild steel plates
1/8" (3.2mm) x 1" (25mm) x 9" (229mm) mild steel backing strip

Electrodes: 3/32" E7018 (Root & 1st Fill Layer)
1/8" E7018 (Fill & Cover Layers)

Polarity: DCEP (Reverse Polarity)

Amperage: 80-100 (for 3/32" E7018 electrodes)
90-150 (for 1/8" E7018 electrodes)

NOTE: *Some machines run hotter than others. Lower amperage may make the puddle easier to control.*

2. Tack Weld and Position Workpiece

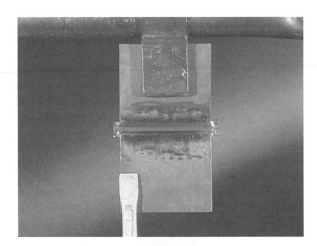

- Bevel each plate 35° to form a 70° included angle.
- Place test plates on top of a 1/8" backing strip and two 1/8" shims. Arrange the plates so the joint is in the center of the backing strip.
- Use 1/4" spacer to form 1/4" root opening and tack weld at both ends of each plate, joining the workpiece to the backing strip.
- Turn the workpiece over and deposit welds along both sides of backing strip to minimize distortion.
- Fixture the workpiece in the horizontal (2G) position

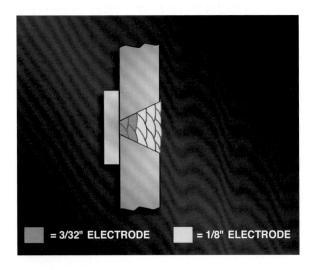

= 3/32" ELECTRODE   = 1/8" ELECTRODE

- This weld involves 5 layers:

  A 2-bead root and first layer using 3/32 inch electrodes with the machine set between 80-100 amps.

  The remaining fill and cover layers using 1/8 inch electrodes with the machine set between 90-150 amps.

 EW369 SMAWA1

3. Deposit Root Pass

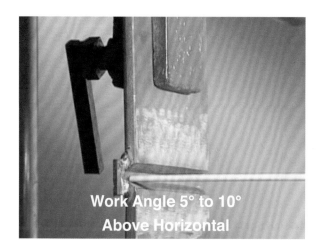

Work Angle 5° to 10° Above Horizontal

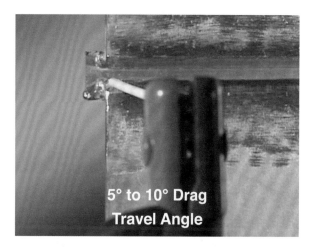

5° to 10° Drag Travel Angle

1st Root Bead

- Center electrode on the bottom plate where the <u>lower</u> bevel meets the backing strip.

- Start the arc using a steady drag.

- Read puddle, travel at a speed to produce a bead 2 to 2-1/2 electrode diameters wide.

- If a **restart** is necessary, clean the slag from crater thoroughly. Position the electrode about 1/2" in front of the crater. Strike the arc and move the electrode back, retrace the crater and resume normal travel.

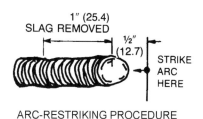

1" (25.4)
SLAG REMOVED
½" (12.7)
STRIKE ARC HERE

ARC-RESTRIKING PROCEDURE

- Finished weld should cover 1/3 to 1/2 of the backing strip and have complete fusion into the bottom bevel.

Work Angle 5° to 10°
Below Horizontal

2nd Root Bead

- Center electrode on the top plate where the <u>upper</u> bevel meets the backing strip.

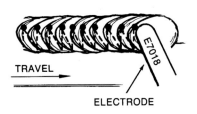

TRAVEL

ELECTRODE

E7018

- Use same 5-10° travel angle with a steady drag
- Travel at a speed to produce a bead about 2 to 2-1/2 electrode diameters wide.
- A slight "W" motion may be needed to flatten and spread the bead.

- The finished root weld should be flat to slightly convex and fills the joint from end to end

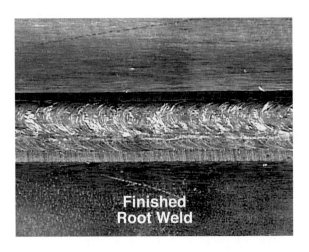

Finished
Root Weld

4. Deposit 1st Fill Layer

- Center the electrode on the lower toe of the root for the **first fill pass**.
- Use a work angle that is 5 to 10-degree <u>above horizontal,</u> with the same 5 to 10-degree drag travel angle.

- Cover the root layer by about 2/3 and melt into the bottom bevel
- For the **second fill pass**, center the electrode on the upper toe of the root pass.
- Use a 5 to 10-degrees <u>below horizontal</u> work angle with the same 5 to 10-degree drag travel angle.

Electrode on the <u>upper</u> toe of the root

- Cover the first fill pass by about a half and melt into the upper bevel. (You may need to use a slight "W" motion to flatten & spread the bead.)

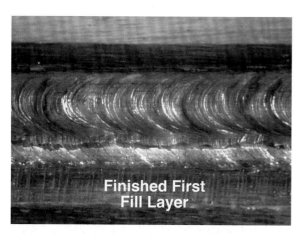

Finished First Fill Layer

The finished layer should have:

- a flat to slightly convex contour that spreads evenly across the joint.
- complete fusion into both bevels
- joint filled out completely from one end of the workpiece to the other.

A common problem is insufficient fill at the upper bevel

If needed, add another fill pass to even out the weld and get a consistant weld with a smooth transition.

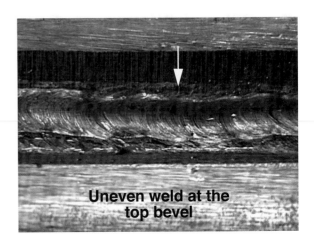

Uneven weld at the top bevel

5. Remaining Fill Layers

- Switch to a 1/8 inch E7018 electrode and increase the amperage.
- Allow the workpiece to cool briefly, or switch to another workpiece.
- Use the same 5 to 10-degree work angle…with the same 5 to 10-degree drag travel angle.

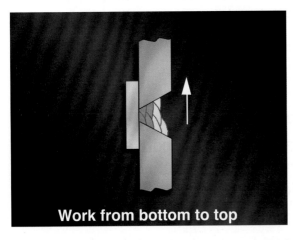

Work from bottom to top

- In the horizontal position…always start at the bottom of the joint and work toward the top to provide support for the next bead in the sequence.
- Use the same electrode angles for each bead in the layers to produce a smooth and even layers.

The finished layers should have:

- a flat to slightly convex contour that spreads evenly across the joint with complete fusion into both bevels
- the joint should be filled out completely from one end of the workpiece to the other.

7. Final Fill and Cover Layers

Final Fill Layer

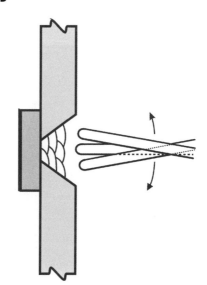

- Allow the workpiece to cool briefly or switch to another workpiece.
- Use the same 5 to 10-degree work angle with the same 5 to 10-degree drag travel angle
- You may need to vary work angles slightly for each bead in order to produce a layer with proper bead overlap.
- Make sure that each weld covers the previous bead by about one-half to 2/3 to produce a smooth contour.
- Finished weld should be flat to slightly convex with complete fusion between the base metal and the weld metal and should fill the joint to within 1/16 inch to the top surface of the base metal.

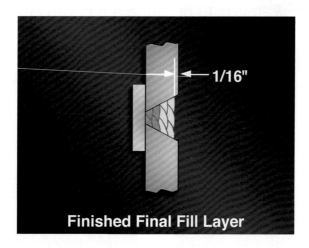

Finished Final Fill Layer

If the distance is more than a 1/16 inch from the weld metal to the surface of the base metal…deposit additional fill passes as necessary, before depositing the cover layer.

Cover Layer

- Allow the workpiece to cool breifly, or switch to another workpiece.

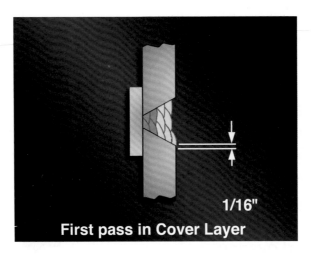

First pass in Cover Layer

1/16"

- Use a drag travel angle of 5 to 10 degrees and a work angle of approximately 90 degrees.
- Melt into the bottom edge of the joint by a sixteenth of an inch to ensure complete fusion.
- Deposit the remaining beads using the same electrode angles
- Make sure that each weld covers the previous bead by about one-half to two-thirds to produce a smooth contour.

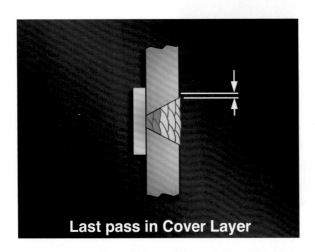

Last pass in Cover Layer

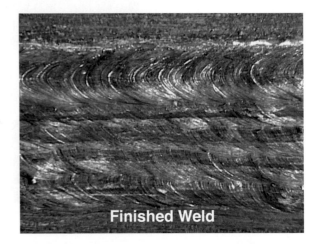

Finished Weld

- The last pass in the cover layer should melt into the top edge of the joint by about a 1/16 inch.

- The finished **Cover Layer** should have a smooth contour and shall be a minimum of flush with the base metal to a maximum of 1/8 inch reinforcement.

- There should be no edge weld undercut or weld bead overlap.

- The weld should have complete fusion into the sides of the joint and previously deposited weld metal.

- The joint must be filled out completely from one end of the workpiece to the other

Inspect welds and continue practice

TOPIC 5

WELD SIZE AND PROFILE

Objective: **To develop a technical understanding of weld size and weld bead profile, in order to produce welds as required by design.**

Introduction

Each welder, regardless of the type of welding required is responsible for the quality, size, and shape of the weld as required by the design.

To be able to produce the type of weld required, the qualified welder must be able to perform certain activities, which include:

- Reading the weld symbol on the blueprint, to determine the size and contour of the required weld.

- Making sure that the joint is set up accurately, and that the base metal surfaces are clean and free of contaminants.

- And reading the weld procedure, to insure that the proper materials and methods are used to produce the weld.

The welder must have a firm grasp of welding techniques that are employed for the various electrodes; and the techniques for controling the molten puddle to produce the required weld.

Fillet Weld Size

Fillet weld size is expressed in terms of leg length. The leg of a fillet weld is the distance from the joint root to the toe. A fillet weld has two leg length dimensions.

The strength of the fillet is determined by the effective size of the weld. This is defined as the length of the largest equal-leg right triangle that can be inscribed within the profile of the weld.

For **convex** or flat equal leg fillet welds, the leg length is equal to the effective size for maximum strength.

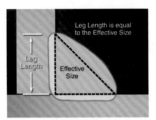

CONVEX FILLET WELD

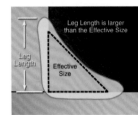

CONCAVE FILLET WELD

For **concave** fillet welds, the leg-length of the weld is slightly larger than the effective size.

When a weld is required to have 1/4 inch long legs, the welder must deposit the weld with equal legs, both 1/4 inch long.

If a weld has one leg that is 1/4 inch long, but the other leg is only 3/16 inch long, then the **effective size** of the weld is reduced to 3/16 inch and the strength of the weld is reduced.

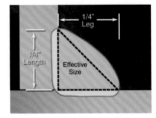

CORRECT SIZE

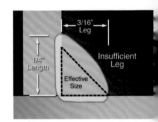

INCORRECT SIZE

When a weld's leg length is less than specified, it is termed **insufficient leg**, and is considered unacceptable

The welder can check the size of the weld by using an instrument called a **fillet weld gauge**.

There are two basic types of fillet weld gauges available; one for measuring **convex fillets**, the other for measuring **concave fillets**.

Convex Fillet Weld Gauge

Convex & Concave Fillet Weld Gauges

Certain fillet weld profiles are considered unacceptable by some welding codes. A weld can be deposited with the proper leg size, yet still be rejected if the weld shows excessive undercut, overlap, or insufficient throat.

COMMON TERMS APPLIED TO FILLET WELDS

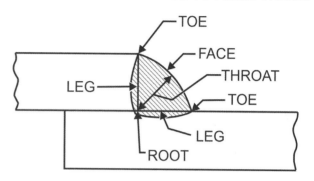

The **throat** of a fillet weld is defined as the distance from the root of a weld to its face, minus any convexity

Sometimes a low spot is produced on the weld face, which reduces the throat. This is commonly the result of improper overlapping on multipass welds.

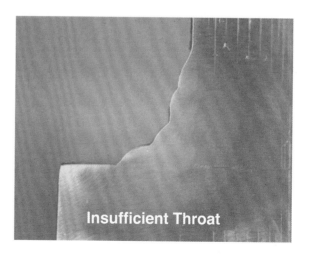

Insufficient Throat

This throat reduction is commonly called **insufficient throat**, which reduces the effective size and the strength of the weld.

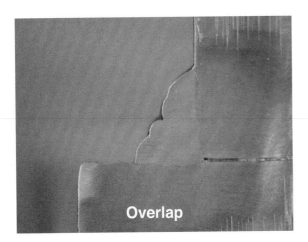
Overlap

Overlap is similar to excessive convexity in that notches are produced along the lower toe.

Overlap is characterized by metal, which extends past the fusion line at the toe of the weld.

Overlap results from too high a welding current or too slow a travel speed.

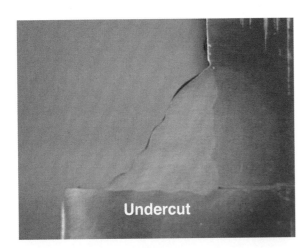
Undercut

Undercut is defined as a groove melted into the base metal at the toe of the weld, and left unfilled. This reduces the base metal thickness at the toe, and produces a notch that concentrates stress.

Undercut results from excessive current setting, or excessive arc length.

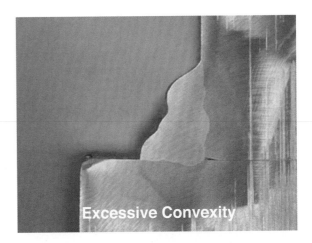
Excessive Convexity

Excessive convexity results from too low a welding current or too fast a travel speed. The amount of permissible convexity is limited by some welding codes, since a notch is produced at the toes of the weld bead, which can concentrate stresses and lead to weld failure.

Groove Weld Size

Unlike fillet welds, which are sized by leg length, the size of a groove weld is defined in terms of joint penetration or groove weld size.

Joint penetration is the minimum depth that a weld extends, from its face into the joint. Joint penetration does not include reinforcement.

Root penetration is metal that penetrates to the root of the joint but not beyond.

Groove welds are categorized into two groups: Complete penetration and partial penetration.

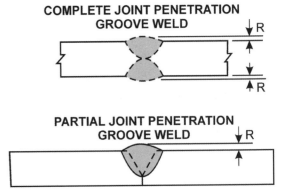
COMPLETE JOINT PENETRATION GROOVE WELD

PARTIAL JOINT PENETRATION GROOVE WELD

R = Reinforcement

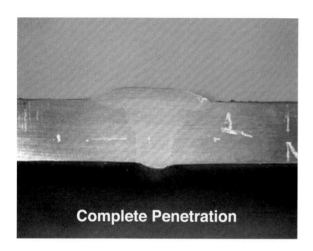
Complete Penetration

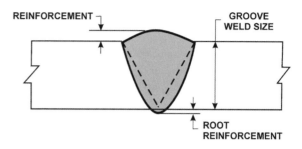

If a weld does not have enough fill to equal the thickness of the joined members, then the weld has **Underfill** and is unacceptable.

Normally, groove welds are made with a slight reinforcement. Typically, for butt joints and corner joints this reinforcement should not exceed the design specifications and should have a gradual transition to the base metal.

Welds that completely fill the groove, and are fused to the base metal throughout the thickness of the joint members, are called complete penetration welds.

For complete penetration welds, the groove weld size is equal to the thickness of the members to be joined.

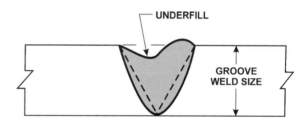

Underfill can result from improper bead sequencing on multipass welds, similar to the case of the fillet weld.

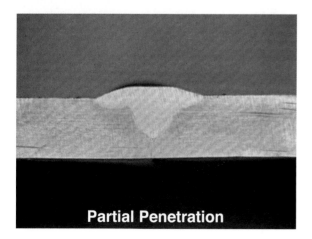
Partial Penetration

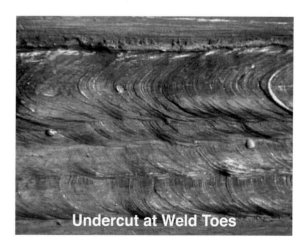
Undercut at Weld Toes

Partial penetration welds do NOT completely penetrate the joint. Some welds are designed this way.

Undercut for groove welds is also similar to fillet welds.

Undercut occurring at the toes of the weld reduce the thickness of the base metal.

Undercut Notches

Excessive Convexiety & Overlap

For groove welds, excessive undercut produces notches, which concentrate stress and can cause weld failure.

Another harmful result of undercut is the increased chance of trapping slag at the toes of multipass welds.

Groove welds should also be free from excessive convexity and overlap. This prevents notches which can concentrate stresses and lead to weld failure.

Slag Entrapment

In conclusion: the welder is responsible for the knowledge and ability to produce fillet and groove welds of the proper size and contour, as required by the design.

EW369 SMAWA1

PROCEDURE & WELDER QUALIFICATION

Objective: To provide an orientation to the requirements of welding codes as they apply to the qualification of welders and procedures.

Introduction

A weld should be suitable for the purpose. The "purpose" may vary from high performance space equipment to a scrap bin.

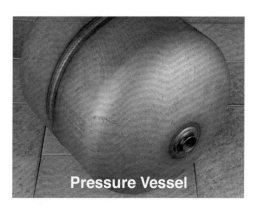
Pressure Vessel

On the other hand, a relatively small flaw in a weld on a pressure vessel could result in much danger to life and equipment.

Welding a Scrap Bin

Quality welds have become common in the welding industry as the result of extensive training, quality control, and procedure refinement.

The cost of producing welds increases as the specified quality of the weld increases.

The cost of the weld must be balanced against safety and other consequences of possible weld failure.

Although a scrap bin may cost only a few dollars and cause no harm if a weld breaks, adequate standards must be maintained if the product is to sell successfully.

Weld Quality

Present day welding technology and welder capability can produce high quality welds.

A weld on a scrap bin may be just as good as a weld on a pressure vessel, and in general, it can be. However, the quality and procedures should not be over specified.

Much of the cost of high quality welding is not in the actual weld itself, but in making sure that it is an adequate weld.

What is a quality weld? How can quality be determined?

> **A quality weld is one that performs without failure under the specified operating conditions of the product.**

Quality can be determined by establishing the required performance from experience or testing, and by setting up a system that will assure that this performance will be maintained.

Welding Codes

For welding the scrap bin, the system would be a list of the basic requirements, with visual inspection.

For more important products, a more thorough procedure is required.

This has led to the development of welding codes... which define the requirements for fabricating various products, such as:

- Bridges and buildings
- Ships
- Storage tanks
- Air and spacecraft
- Construction equipment
- Pipe and Piping construction

Fortunately, there is much similarity in welding specifications among the various codes.

The three most widely used codes are:

- The ASME Boiler and Pressure Vessel Code
- API Standard for Welding Pipelines and Related facilities
- The AWS Structural Welding Code

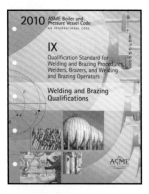

All of these welding codes require qualifying procedures and qualified welders.

Welding Procedure Specification

A **Welding Procedure** gives the step-by-step directions for making a specific weld or weldment, which will meet the service requirements of the product. It establishes standards high enough to assure a quality result without requiring excessive cost.

You may never be required to prepare a **Welding Procedure Specification (WPS),** since this is usually the job of others.

However, you will likely be required to prepare the welds for a welding procedure specification, or for your own qualification.

In a typical situation, a manufacturer will prepare a welding procedure specification for the weldment.

A welder will be called on to make the welds as specified in the welding procedure...

Non-Destructive Testing

The weld samples will then be tested by either destructive or non-destructive testing. If the samples pass the test, the welding procedure specification is qualified...*and so is the welder who prepared the samples.*

Destructive Test Specemins

Additional welders may be qualified by preparing and successfully testing similar weld samples.

A welding procedure specification according to the American Society of Mechanical Engineers Boiler and Pressure Vessel Code, can be prepared on forms available from the Society or on company-prepared forms.

A simple example for a vee groove butt joint would contain:

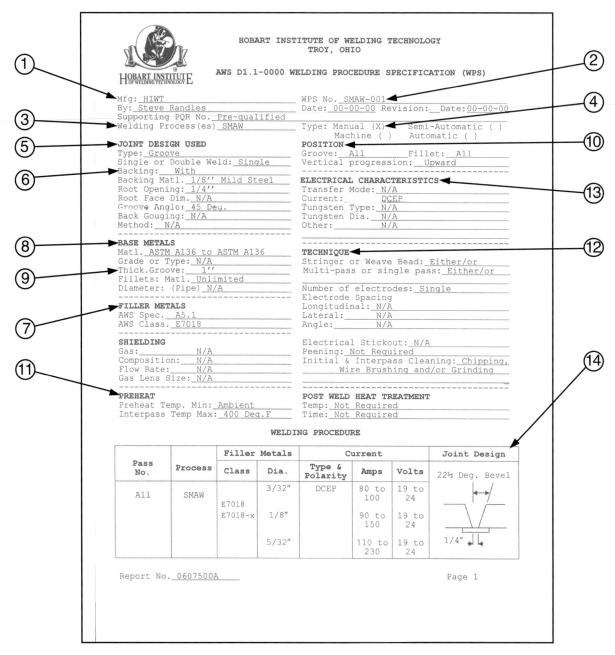

HOBART INSTITUTE OF WELDING TECHNOLOGY
TROY, OHIO

AWS D1.1-0000 WELDING PROCEDURE SPECIFICATION (WPS)

① Mfg: HIWT
By: Steve Randles
③ Supporting PQR No. Pre-qualified
Welding Process(es) SMAW

② WPS No. SMAW-001
Date: 00-00-00 Revision: Date:00-00-00

④ Type: Manual (X) Semi-Automatic ( )
Machine ( ) Automatic ( )

⑤ **JOINT DESIGN USED**
Type: Groove
Single or Double Weld: Single
⑥ Backing: With
Backing Matl. 1/8'' Mild Steel
Root Opening: 1/4''
Root Face Dim. N/A
Groove Angle: 45 Deg.
Back Gouging: N/A
Method: N/A

⑩ **POSITION**
Groove: All   Fillet: All
Vertical progression: Upward

⑬ **ELECTRICAL CHARACTERISTICS**
Transfer Mode: N/A
Current: DCEP
Tungsten Type: N/A
Tungsten Dia. N/A
Other: N/A

⑧ **BASE METALS**
Matl. ASTM A136 to ASTM A136
Grade or Type: N/A
⑨ Thick.Groove: 1''
Fillets: Matl. Unlimited
Diameter: (Pipe) N/A

⑫ **TECHNIQUE**
Stringer or Weave Bead: Either/or
Multi-pass or single pass: Either/or

Number of electrodes: Single
Electrode Spacing
Longitudinal: N/A
Lateral: N/A
Angle: N/A

⑦ **FILLER METALS**
AWS Spec. A5.1
AWS Class. E7018

SHIELDING
Gas: N/A
Composition: N/A
Flow Rate: N/A
Gas Lens Size: N/A

Electrical Stickout: N/A
Peening: Not Required
Initial & Interpass Cleaning: Chipping,
Wire Brushing and/or Grinding

⑪ **PREHEAT**
Preheat Temp. Min: Ambient
Interpass Temp Max: 400 Deg.F

POST WELD HEAT TREATMENT
Temp: Not Required
Time: Not Required

WELDING PROCEDURE

| Pass No. | Process | Filler Metals | | Current | | | Joint Design |
		Class	Dia.	Type & Polarity	Amps	Volts	
All	SMAW	E7018 E7018-x	3/32"	DCEP	80 to 100	19 to 24	22½ Deg. Bevel
			1/8"		90 to 150	19 to 24	
			5/32"		110 to 230	19 to 24	1/4"

⑭

Report No. 0607500A

Page 1

1. The company name

2. Identifying numbers

3. Welding process

4. Type or method

5. Joint groove design

6. Backing

7. Filler metal

8. Base Metal

9. Thickness range.

10. Position and progression

11. Preheat requirements

12. Technique

13. Electrical characteristics

14. A sketch of the joint.

Now, to qualify the procedures, an additional form is completed which identifies and records the results of various tests, such as: a tensile test and guided bend test.

Other tests may be specified also, such as a toughness test, or a fillet weld soundness test.

Once qualified, you may continue to work on this job without re-qualifying…

Although, re-qualifying is required if changes are made in the specifications, or if you have not welded for several months.

If you maintain your skill, you will be able to qualify when the need arises.

The important thing to remember is that every weld should be made according to established procedures to the best of your ability.

The performance of a weld is a result of contributions by management, designers, production specialists, quality control... and very importantly...the welder.

HOBART INSTITUTE OF WELDING TECHNOLOGY
Troy, Ohio

WELDER QUALIFICATION TEST RECORD

Welder Name: _Steven Randles_   Type: _Welder_   I.D.# _____
WPS No.: _SMAW-001_   Rev.: _-_   Date _-_   Test Date: _00-00-0000_

The Above Welder Is Qualified For The Following Ranges:

Variables	Record Actual Values Used in Qualification	Qualification Range
Process/Type	SMAW	Same
Electrode (single or multiple)	Single	Same
Current/Polarity	D.C.E.P.	Same
Position	3G	Flat,Horz,Vert
Weld Progression	Upward	Same
Backing	With	Same
Material/Spec.	ASTM A36 to ASTM A36	Group I or II
Base Metal		
Thickness:(plate)		
Groove	1.000"	.125" to Unltd.
Fillet	N/A	.125" to Unltd.
Thickness:(pipe/tube)		
Groove	N/A	.125" to Unltd.
Fillet	N/A	.125" to Unltd.
Diameter:(pipe)		
Groove	N/A	Over 24" Dia.
Fillet	N/A	Unlimited
Filler Metal		
Spec. No.	AWS A5.1	Same
Class	E7018	See WPS
F-No.	F4	See WPS
Gas/Flux Type	N/A	Same
Flow Rate	N/A	Same

Guided Bend Test Results

Type	Results	Type	Results
3G Side Bend	Conforms	3G Side Bend	Conforms

Visual Inspection: _Conforms to AWS D1.1 Structural Welding Code-Steel_

Fillet Weld Test Results

Appearance _N/A_   Fillet Size: _N/A_
Fracture Test Root Penetration _N/A_   Macroetch's _N/A_
(Describe the location, nature, and size of any crack or tearing of specimen)

Radiographic Test Results

Film Identification No. _N/A_   Results _N/A_   Remarks _N/A_

Test Conducted By: _Hobart Institute_   Report No: _0607500B_

Per: _____   Date: _____
We, the undersigned, certify that the statements in this record are correct and that the test welds were prepared, welded, and tested in accordance with the requirements of Section 4 of ANSI/AWS D1.1, (XXXX) Structural Welding Code-Steel.
Manufacturer or Contractor: _Hobart Institute of Welding Technology_

Authorized By: _____   Date: _____

Weld Qualification Record

Objective: To produce a quality multi-pass single V-groove weld on 3/8-inch mild steel in the horizontal ...or 2G position with a backing strip, that passes a visual inspection and a guided bend test.

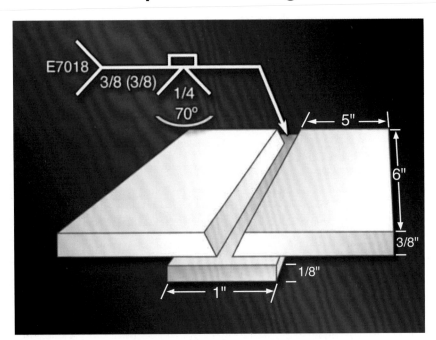

1. Materials & Machine Settings

Base Metal: 3/8" (9.5mm) x 5" (127mm) x 6" (152mm) mild steel plates
1/8" (3.2mm) x 1" (25mm) x 9" (229mm) mild steel backing strip

Electrodes: 3/32" E7018 (Root & 1st Fill Layer)
1/8" E7018 (Fill & Cover Layers)

Polarity: DCEP (Reverse Polarity)

Amperage: 80-100 (Root & 1st Fill Layer)
90-150 (Fill & Cover Layers)

NOTE: *Some machines run hotter than others. Lower amperage may make the puddle easier to control.*

2. Prepare Workpiece & Weld

Prepare a single V-groove weld in a butt joint using a set of test plates by following the instructions given in topic 4.

3. Visual Inspection

Cracks

A weld shall be acceptable by visual inspection if it shows that the weld has no cracks; otherwise, it shall be considered as having failed.

Cracks

Fusion

A weld shall be acceptable by visual inspection if it shows that there is complete fusion between weld metal and base metal, as well as with previously deposited weld metal; otherwise, it shall be considered as having failed.

Incomplete Fusion

Slag Inclusions

A weld shall be acceptable by visual inspection if there is no slag inclusion that exceeds 1/8" in any 6 inches of weld; otherwise, it shall be considered as having failed.

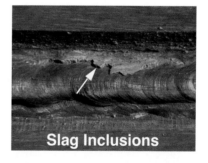
Slag Inclusions

Undercut

A weld shall be acceptable by visual inspection if undercut does not exceed 1/32" wide, 1/32" deep and has no more than the combined total of 2" of undercut in any 6 inches of weld.

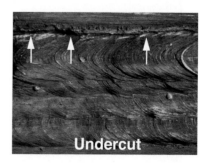
Undercut

Porosity

A weld shall be acceptable by visual inspection if porosity does not exceed 1/16" maximum and has no more than the combined total of 1/8" in any one square inch of weld; otherwise, it shall be considered as having failed.

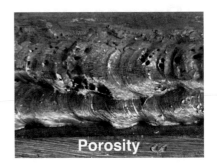
Porosity

Overlap

The weld shall be acceptable if there is no overlap. Overlap (cold lap) occurs when the weld metal rolls up on the base metal or previously deposited weld metal without fusion.

Overlap

Reinforcement

A weld shall be acceptable by visual inspection if the face reinforcement does not exceed the specified dimension, and shows a gradual transition of the surface of the base metal. Any reinforcement must blend smoothly into the plate or previous weld surface, with transition areas free from edge weld undercut.

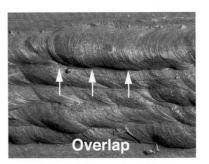
Reinforcement

1/8" Maximum Reinforcement

For this single V-groove weld the face reinforcement shall be a minimum of flush with the base metal, to a maximum of 1/8 inch, otherwise it shall be considered as having failed.

3. Prepare and Bend Test Samples

- Mark the 2 test straps, and stamp face and root identification on them.

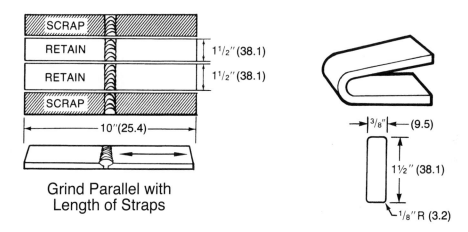

Grind Parallel with
Length of Straps

- Cut the straps and discard the two end pieces.

- Remove backing strip from each specimen by grinding.

> *Always grind a test specimen along its length. If you grind across the specimen, grind marks in the weld could cause it to fail.*

- On each strap, grind both surfaces of the weld flush with the plate. Do not remove base metal.
- Bend one strap root side down, and the other face side down, in a guided bend jig.

Standards of Acceptability

The convex surface of the specimen shall contain no discontinuities exceeding the following dimensions:

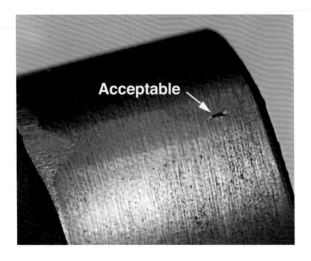 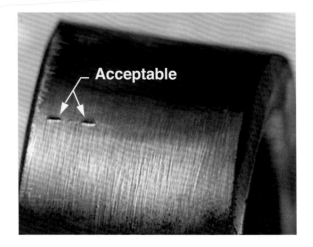

1/8" (3.2mm) measured in any direction on the surface.

A sum of 3/8" (9.5mm) of the greatest dimensions of all discontinuities exceeding 1/32" but less than or equal to 1/8".

Analyze test results and check with your instructor.

Objective: To produce a quality multi-pass single V-groove weld in the vertical...or 3G position with a backing strip, that passes a visual inspection and guided bend test.

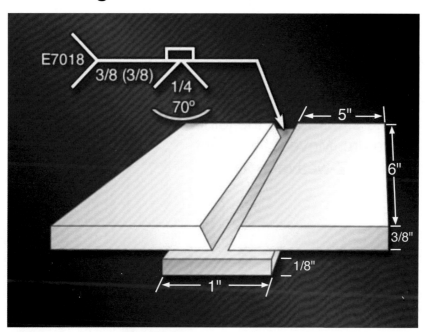

1. Materials & Machine Settings

Base Metal: 3/8" (9.5mm) x 5" (127mm) x 6" (152mm) mild steel plates
1/8" (3.2mm) x 1" (25mm) x 9" (229mm) mild steel backing strip

Electrodes: 3/32" E7018 (Root & 1st Fill Layer)
1/8" E7018 (Fill & Cover Layers)

Polarity: DCEP (Reverse Polarity)

Amperage: 80-100 (Root & 1st Fill Layer)
90-150 (Fill & Cover Layers)

NOTE: *Some machines run hotter than others. Lower amperage may make the puddle easier to control.*

2. Tack Weld & Position Workpiece

- Bevel two 3/8" plates with 35 degree angles and assemble a workpiece using the instructions given in Topic 4.
- Clamp in vertical (3G) position.

3. Deposit Root Pass

- Using a 3/32 inch E7018 electrode, center the electrode in the joint and strike the arc. Move up the joint with a slight Z-weave motion.

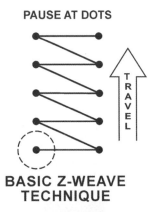

PAUSE AT DOTS

TRAVEL

BASIC Z-WEAVE TECHNIQUE

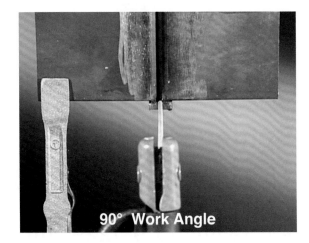

90° Work Angle

90° to 5° Push Travel Angle

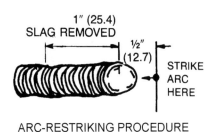

1" (25.4)
SLAG REMOVED

½"
(12.7)

STRIKE
ARC
HERE

ARC-RESTRIKING PROCEDURE

- If a **restart** is necessary, clean the slag from crater thoroughly. Position the electrode about 1/2" in front of the crater. Strike the arc and move the electrode back, retrace the crater and resume normal travel.

- The finished fill layer should be flat to slightly convex with complete fusion into both bevels and must fill the joint from one end of the workpiece to the other.

4. First Fill Layer

- Same electrode and amp settings as for the root pass.
- Use the same 90° work angle and the same 90° to 5° push travel angle
- Beginning at either toe, travel up joint with Z-weave technique. Pause briefly at each toe and move up joint to produce a bead about 1/2" wide.

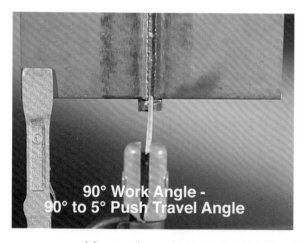

- Keep the electrode in the front third of the puddle, then adjust your travel speed, angles and electrode position to produce a consistent weld with a smooth transition into the base metal.
- Finished layer should completely cover the root pass and have complete fusion into both bevels.

5. Remaining Fill Layers

- Switch to a 1/8 inch E7018 electrode and increase the amperage.
- Allow the workpiece to cool briefly, or switch to another workpiece.
- Use the same 90° work angle and the same 90° to 5° push travel angle.

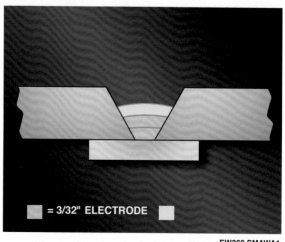

The finished layers should have:

- a flat to slightly convex contour that spreads evenly across the joint.

- complete fusion into both bevels

- joint filled out completely from   one end of the workpiece to the other.

6. Final Fill and Cover Layers

Final Fill Layer

- Allow the workpiece to cool briefly or switch to another workpiece.

- Use the same 90° work angle and the same 90° to 5° push travel angle

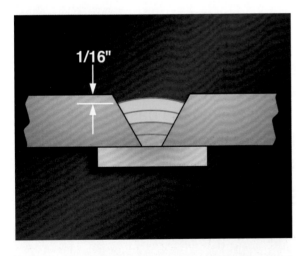

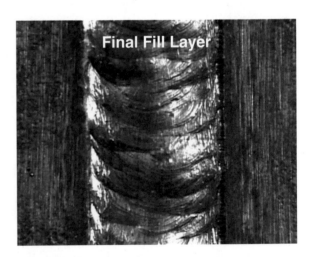

- Finished weld should be flat to slightly convex with complete fusion between the base metal and the weld metal and should fill the joint to within 1/16 inch to the top surface of the base metal.

> *If the distance is more than a 1/16 inch, deposit additional fill passes as necessary, before depositing the cover layer.*

Cover Layer

- Let the workpiece cool briefly…Then use the same electrode angles to deposit the cover pass.

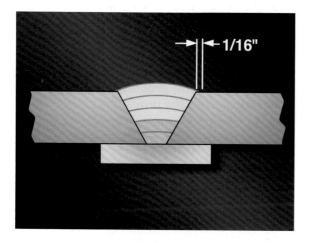

- The finished weld should melt into the bevel edges by about 1/16 inch, have a smooth contour and shall be a minimum of flush with the base metal to a maximum of 1/8 inch reinforcement.

- There should be no edge weld undercut or weld bead overlap and with complete fusion into the sides of the joint.

- The joint must be filled out completely from one end of the workpiece to the other.

Inspect welds and continue practice

DESTRUCTIVE TESTING

Objective: To define destructive testing, and to present a brief description of the different testing methods.

Introduction

Many welding codes use a variety of destructive testing methods, to establish design-performance requirements and to qualify welding procedures and welders.

> They are called **destructive tests** because the test specimen is broken or permanently damaged during testing.

The test specimen is always prepared from the same materials and welded with the same procedure that will be used to fabricate the final weldment.

Destructive testing is a function performed by quality control to maintain the expected weldment reliability during service.

Often, after the design is proven through destructive testing, no further qualification or testing is required for production of the actual weldment. However, qualified welding procedures and visual inspection are used to assure the continuing quality of the weldment.

When code requirements must be met, a careful study of the specified destructive tests is required.

> *As a welder, your job will probably only demand that you produce a sound weld as specified by the procedures.*

Guided Bend Test

The **Guided Bend Test** is where a specimen is bent into a U shape to determine the soundness of a weld.

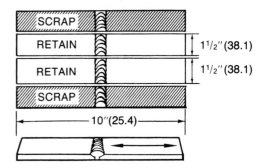

Generally, specimens are cut from the middle of the workpiece. Once the specimen has been cut and properly ground, it is placed in a bending fixture and bent into a U shape.

After bending, the convex surface of the specimens are visually inspected for discontinuities.

Side Bend Test

Another test is the **Side Bend Test**. In this test, 3/8-inch wide specimens are cut about 1" from each side of the centerline of the workpiece.

The specimens are ground, bent into a U shape and then the convex surface is visually inspected for discontinuities to determine the soundness of the weld.

The side bend test is commonly used when the thickness of the material is greater than 3/8".

Tensile Test

With a tensile test, material is subjected to a pulling stress in order to accurately determine the tensile strength of a weld or base metal.

After the sample welds have been made in accordance with the Welding Procedure Specification (WPS), specimens are then machined to be either flat or round specimens.

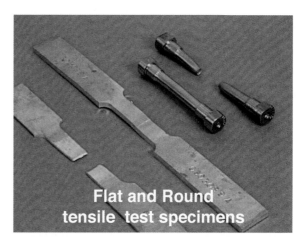

Flat and Round tensile test specimens

Flat samples are narrowed in the weld area, and then pulled to the breaking point.

Round samples are commonly used when testing all weld metal. The entire necked-down or reduced section consists entirely of weld metal.

The location from which the tensile specimens are removed from the sample should be outlined in the testing procedure.

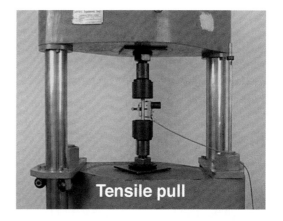

Tensile pull

Once the specimen has been prepared, it is pulled to the breaking point in a tensile pull machine.

For acceptance, the specimen must withstand or exceed its rated tensile strength.

Nick-Break Test

For this test, a specimen normally one inch wide is cut out of a weld.

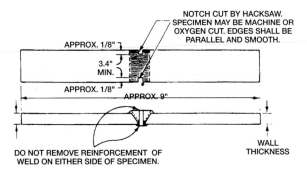

NOTCH CUT BY HACKSAW. SPECIMEN MAY BE MACHINE OR OXYGEN CUT. EDGES SHALL BE PARALLEL AND SMOOTH.

APPROX. 1/8"

3.4" MIN.

APPROX. 1/8"

APPROX. 9"

WALL THICKNESS

DO NOT REMOVE REINFORCEMENT OF WELD ON EITHER SIDE OF SPECIMEN.

It is then notched at each end of the weld metal and is subjected to a impact force or blow until the specimen is broken. The interior of the weld is then visually inspected for poor fusion, slag inclusions and porosity.

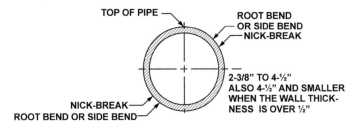

TOP OF PIPE

ROOT BEND OR SIDE BEND

NICK-BREAK

NICK-BREAK

ROOT BEND OR SIDE BEND

2-3/8" TO 4-½" ALSO 4-½" AND SMALLER WHEN THE WALL THICK-NESS IS OVER ½"

In pipe welding, the nick-break specimens are taken from the pipe at specific points. The type and number of specimens vary with the size of the pipe, according to the welding code being used. The acceptability of the weld is usually based on the specific welding code.

Fillet Weld Break Test

Another type of mechanical soundness test is the fillet weld break test. With this test, a fillet weld is deposited in a tee joint and then broken. The interior of the weld is visually inspected for:

- poor fusion
- slag inclusions
- porosity

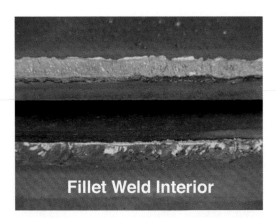

Fillet Weld Interior

The finished fillet weld can be flattened in a press or struck with a hammer until the weld breaks.

The size of the base metal and the fillet weld depends on the welding code or procedure being used.

The fillet weld break test is often used to evaluate and qualify tack-welders for the structural welding industry.

Macroetch Test

Another type of destructive test is the Macroetch Test. A cross-section is cut from a weld, and the specimen is then ground to a smooth polished finish.

Macroetch specimen

A special acid is then used to etch the metal. The acid helps show the weld structure and presence of any defects more clearly

An acceptable weld should have proper fusion, penetration, and leg size. There shouldn't be any cracks, porosity, or slag inclusions.

Charpy V-notch Test

The Charpy Impact test... also referred to as the Charpy V-notch is another type of mechanical destructive test.

Here, a test specimen is taken perpendicular to the weld axis, carefully machined to a rectangular cross-section, and notched in the center of the weld area.

This test is widely used by most codes and the dimensions of the prepared test specimen are almost always identical.

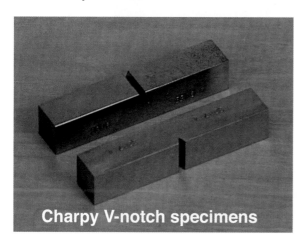

Charpy V-notch specimens

The amount of impact energy is indicated on a gauge in foot-pounds.

The part's resistance to breakage is a measure of the material's ability to withstand sudden force or shock loads.

The sample is then clamped firmly into a special machine and a weighted arm is allowed to strike the piece until the piece breaks.

Broken test specimens

> For the weld to be acceptable, the results must fall within the impact strength range for that type of material.

Charpy V-notch Process

In your career as a welder, you will probably make many welds for test purposes.

Your part will be to make the best weld possible under the conditions specified.

The resulting weld should pass the test.

SINGLE V-GROOVE WELD, BUTT JOINT, OVERHEAD (4G) POSITION

Objective: To produce a quality multi-pass single V-groove weld in the overhead…or 4G position with a backing strip, that passes a visual inspection and guided bend test.

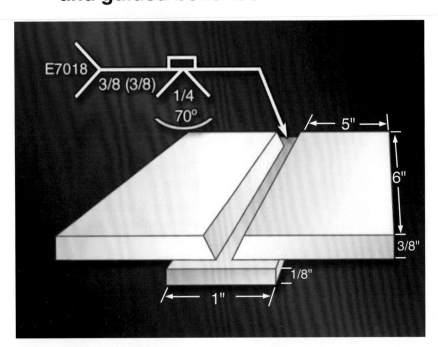

1. Materials & Machine Settings

Base Metal: 3/8" (9.5mm) x 5" (127mm) x 6" (152mm) mild steel plates
1/8" (3.2mm) x 1" (25mm) x 9" (229mm) mild steel backing strip

Electrodes: 3/32" E7018 (Root & 1st Fill Layer)
1/8" E7018 (Fill & Cover Layers)

Polarity: DCEP (Reverse Polarity)

Amperage: 80-100 (Root & 1st Fill Layer)
90-150 (Fill & Cover Layers)

NOTE: *Some machines run hotter than others. Lower amperage may make the puddle easier to control.*

2. Tack Weld & Position Workpiece

- Bevel two 3/8" plates with 35 degree angles and assemble a workpiece using the instructions given in Topic 4.
- Clamp in overhead (4G) position.

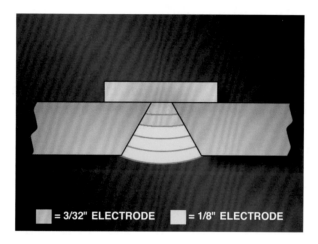

= 3/32" ELECTRODE   = 1/8" ELECTRODE

- This weld involves 5 layers. The actual bead count may vary depending on weld size, bead placement and other factors such as root opening and bevel angle.

90° Work Angle

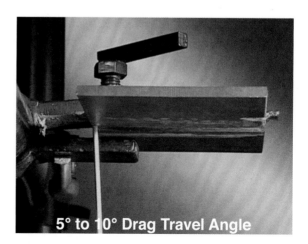

5° to 10° Drag Travel Angle

- Using a 3/32 inch E7018 electrode, center the electrode in the joint and strike the arc. Move up the joint with a slight Z-weave motion.

- If a **restart** is necessary, clean the slag from crater thoroughly. Position the electrode about 1/2" in front of the crater. Strike the arc and move the electrode back, retrace the crater and resume normal travel.

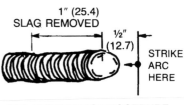

1" (25.4)
SLAG REMOVED
½"
(12.7)
STRIKE ARC HERE

ARC-RESTRIKING PROCEDURE

- Finished weld should be flat to slightly convex and have complete fusion into both bevels. The joint must be filled out from one end of the workpiece to the other.

4. First Fill Layer

- Same electrode and amp settings as for the root pass.
- Use the same 90° work angle and the same 5° to 10° drag travel angle
- Beginning at either toe, use a Z-weave motion and move across the joint to produce a bead about 1/2" wide.

90° Work Angle

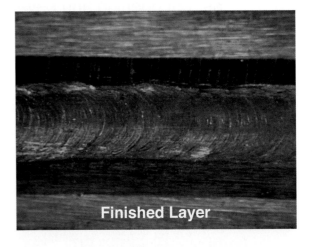

Finished Layer

- Keep the electrode in the front third of the puddle, then adjust your travel speed, angles and electrode position to produce a consistent weld with a smooth transition into the base metal.
- The finished fill layer should be flat to slightly convex with complete fusion into both bevels. Fill the joint from one end of the workpiece to the other.

5. Remaining Fill Layers

- Switch to a 1/8 inch E7018 electrode and increase the amperage.
- Allow the workpiece to cool briefly, or switch to another workpiece.
- Use the same 90° work angle and the same 5° to 10° drag travel angle.
- Use the same electrode angles and techniques for the remaining fill layers

PAUSE AT DOTS

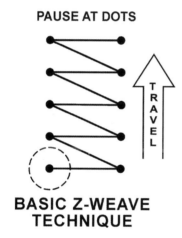

**BASIC Z-WEAVE
TECHNIQUE**

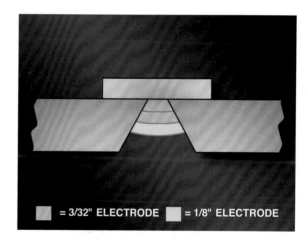

■ = 3/32" ELECTRODE □ = 1/8" ELECTRODE

The finished layers should have:

- a flat to slightly convex contour that spreads evenly across the joint.
- complete fusion into both bevels
- joint filled out completely from   one end of the workpiece to the other.

5. Final Fill and Cover Layers

Final Fill Layer

- Allow the workpiece to cool briefly or switch to another workpiece.

- Use the same 90° work angle and the same 5° to 10° drag travel angle.

- Finished weld should be flat to slightly convex with complete fusion between the base metal and the weld metal and should fill the joint to within 1/16 inch to the top surface of the base metal.

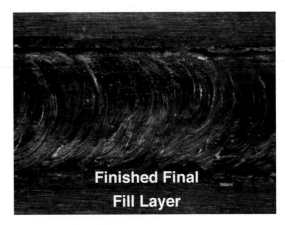

**Finished Final
Fill Layer**

- The weld should fill the joint from one end of the workpiece to the other.

If the distance is more than a 1/16 inch from the weld metal to the surface of the base metal, deposit additional fill passes as necessary, before depositing the cover layer.

Cover Layer

- Let the workpiece cool briefly…Then use the same electrode angles to deposit the cover pass.

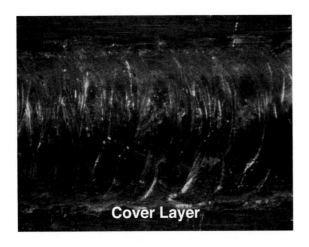

Cover Layer

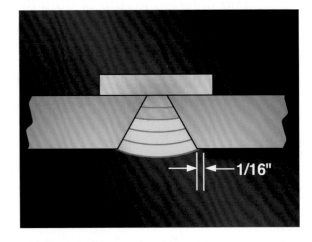

1/16"

- The finished weld should melt into the bevel edges by about 1/16 inch have a smooth contour and shall be a minimum of flush with the base metal to a maximum of 1/8 inch reinforcement.
- There should be no weld edge undercut or overlap. The weld shall have complete fusion into the sides of the joint and the joint must be filled out completely from one end of the workpiece to the other.

Inspect welds and continue practice

NONDESTRUCTIVE TESTING

Objective: **To define the function and meaning of nondestructive testing, and to present a brief description of the different methods.**

Introduction

The use of quality control, welding procedures and destructive testing of weld samples are the foundation for good weldments. With most welding requirements, this will provide all the reliability that is needed.

In certain cases however, some welded products require a greater assurance for reliability. Sometimes regulations demand a higher degree of quality and therefore require more stringent testing to assure weld quality and expose any hidden defects or flaws.

> Non**destructive tests** detect flaws or discontinuties in materials without damaging or impairing the parts usefullness.

NondestructiveTesting

The four most commonly used nondestructive tests are:

- Liquid penetrant
- Magnetic particle
- Radiographic
- Ultrasonic.

Each of these techniques have specific advantages, disadvantages and limitations. We will cover most basic and most commonly used here.

Liquid Penetrant

Liquid penetrant inspection (also reffered to as Visible Dye) is very sensitive. It can detect very small cracks and holes, which are open to the surface, yet are almost invisible to visual inspection.

Before applying the dye, the part must be free of paint or slag and then carefully cleaned.

The dye, usually red in color, is applied to the part and allowed to soak into holes or cracks that may exist.

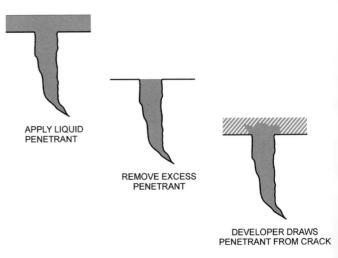

APPLY LIQUID PENETRANT

REMOVE EXCESS PENETRANT

DEVELOPER DRAWS PENETRANT FROM CRACK

The excess dye is then removed with a solvent and then the part is sprayed with a developer.

Defect appears in developer

As any remaining dye soaks into the developer, the defect can now be detected as it appears larger than it actually is.

Florescent penetrant

With florescent penentrant testing, ultraviolet light is used instead of white powder developer to detect the flaw.

Florescent penetrant application

When used in a darkened room, the ultraviolet or "black light" causes the defective area to appear as a brilliant yellowish green. The remaining surface appears deep violet.

Fluorescent inspection is considered even more sensitive than visible dye penetrant.

Magnetic Particle Inspection

Magnetic Particle Inspection is most commonly used on ferrous metals that can be magnetized, such as iron and steel. This process will detect surface cracks and flaws that are slightly under the surface of the magnetized part.

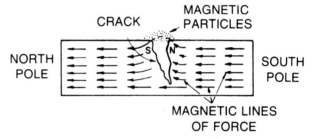

For example, if small magnetic particles are placed on a bar-shaped magnet, they will cling to the magnet only at each end. (The north and south poles.)

Magnetic particles on magnet

If the magnet is cracked, the magnetic lines of force must pass through the air at the crack, creating north and south poles at the sides of the crack. Therefore, when magnetic particles are applied, they will be attracted to the crack.

**Surface flaw -
Magnetic particle test**

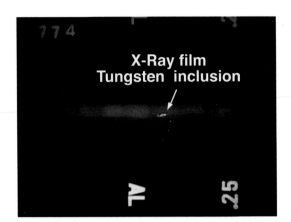

**X-Ray film
Tungsten inclusion**

When the part being tested is magnetized by placing it in a strong magnetic field, the part will act like the magnet.

So, if a surface flaw or a flaw slightly under the surface is present, it will attract and hold small metal particles that are placed on it, roughly in the shape of the flaw.

Radiographic Testing

Radiographic testing uses X-ray or gamma radiation to examine the interior of a material. It provides a permanent record on film and can identify porosity, inclusions, cracks, and other discontinuities within the weld metal.

The process is similar to X-rays used to detect broken bones.

Flaws such as imbedded slag, holes, or cracks, allow more rays to pass through, and cause a darker spot on the film which appear when the film is developed in a darkroom. Tungsten inclusions will appear as white spots on the film due to their density.

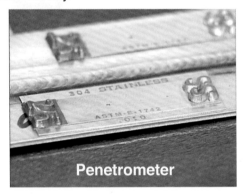

Penetrometer

A thin plate with small holes in it, called a penetrometer, is used to determine the image quality. The clarity of the smallest hole of the penetrometer indicates the clarity of the film image.

Radiographic testing is a popular method of checking for internal flaws on all types of material. It is an expensive method, but one of the most accurate.

> *Advancements in X-ray imaging has led to development of Industrial Digital Radiography (DIR). Digital Radiography offers many benefits over traditional X-ray testing. For example, the detectors can record a digital image which allows the X-ray image inspected and stored using a computer. This eliminates the need for a darkroom, films and chemicals used in traditional X-ray imaging.*

Ultrasonic Testing

Ultrasonic testing makes use of sound waves created by mechanical vibration to locate, measure, and identify flaws.

These sound waves are sent and received by special instruments and cannot be heard by human ears.

The equipment is portable, and can be used on any solid material.

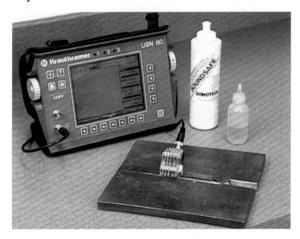

By using a device called a transducer, sound waves can be sent into a solid object such as a weld sample, where they travel to the opposite side and bounce back to the starting point.

The difference in time for the sound waves to return shows up on a small digital screen as a distance-measurement.

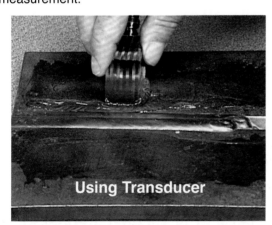

Using Transducer

If we have a sample block and pass sound waves through it, the digital read-out would show two peaks in a line.

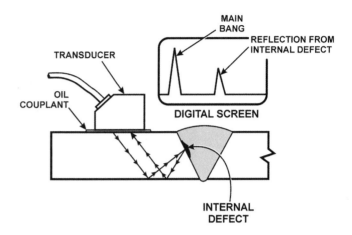

The height of the peak indicates the size of the flaw; and the position of the peak indicates the depth.

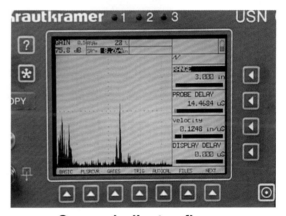

Screen indicates flaws

Quality work by the welder is the most important part of every welding job. Nondestructive testing can help assure that welds are of high-quality and contain no hidden flaws.

Objective: To produce quality multi-pass single V-groove welds in the horizontal... or 2G position with a backing strip.

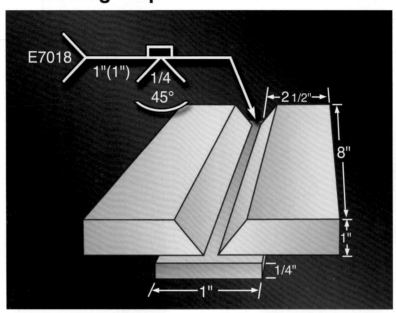

1. Materials & Machine Settings

Base Metal: 1" (25mm) x 2 1/2" (63.5mm) x 8" (203mm) mild steel plates
1/4" (6.35mm) x 1" (25mm) x 10" (254mm) mild steel backing strip

Electrodes: 3/32" E7018 (Root & 1st Fill Layer)
1/8" E7018 (Fill & Cover Layers)
5/32" E7018 (Optional Fill & Cover Layers)

Polarity: DCEP (Reverse Polarity)

Amperage: 80-100 (Root & 1st Fill Layer)
90-150 (Fill & Cover Layers)
110-230 (Optional Fill & Cover Layers)

NOTE: *Some machines run hotter than others. Lower amperage may make the puddle easier to control.*

2. Tack Weld and Position Workpiece

- Bevel each plate 22-1/2° to form a 45° included angle.
- Place test plates on top of a 1/4" backing strip and two 1/4" shims. Arrange the plates so the joint is in the center of the backing strip.
- Use 1/4" spacer to form 1/4" root opening and tack weld at both ends of each plate, joining the workpiece to the backing strip.
- Turn the workpiece over and deposit welds along both sides of backing strip to minimize distortion.

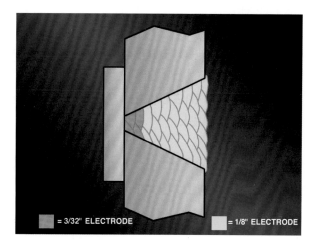

= 3/32" ELECTRODE   = 1/8" ELECTRODE

- Add a tab to the workpiece and then fixture the workpiece in the horizontal (2G) position

3. Deposit Root Pass

Work Angle 5° to 10°
Above Horizontal

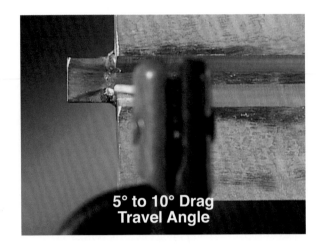

5° to 10° Drag
Travel Angle

First Root Bead

- Center the 3/32 inch electrode on the bottom plate where the lower bevel meets the backing strip.

- Start the arc and move along the joint with a steady drag.

- *Read the puddle* - travel at a speed to produce a bead 2 to 2-1/2 electrode diameters wide. Keep the electrode in the front third of the puddle.

- If a **restart** is necessary, clean the slag from crater thoroughly. Position the electrode about 1/2" in front of the crater. Strike the arc and move the electrode back, retrace the crater and resume normal travel.

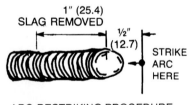

ARC-RESTRIKING PROCEDURE

- Finished weld should cover 1/3 to 1/2 the backing strip and have complete fusion into the bottom bevel.

Work Angle 5° to 10°
Below Horizontal

Second Root Bead

- Center electrode on the top plate where the <u>upper</u> bevel meets the backing strip.

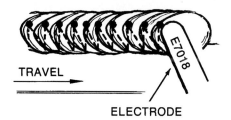

TRAVEL

ELECTRODE

E7018

- Use same 5-10° travel angle with a steady drag

- Travel at a speed to produce a bead about 2 to 2-1/2 electrode diameters wide.

- The weld should melt into the bevel and cover the first root pass by about 1/2 to 2/3.

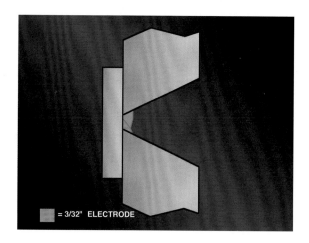

= 3/32" ELECTRODE

- A slight "W" motion may be needed to flatten and spread the bead.

- The finished root weld should be flat to slightly convex and fills the joint from end to end.

EW369 SMAWA1

4. Deposit First Fill Layer

- For the **first fill pass**, center the 3/32 inch electrode on the lower toe of the root layer.
- Use a 5 to 10-degrees <u>above horizontal</u> work angle…with the same 5 to 10-degree drag travel angle.

Electrode on the <u>lower</u> toe of the root

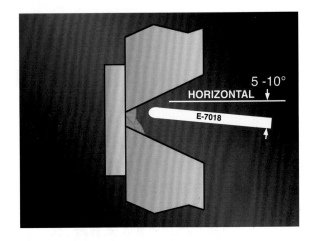

5 -10°
HORIZONTAL
E-7018

- Cover the root layer by about 1/2 to 2/3 and melt into the bottom bevel. A slight "W" motion may be needed to flatten & spread the bead.
- For the **second fill pass**, center the electrode on the upper toe of the root pass.
- Use a 5 to 10-degrees <u>below horizontal</u> work angle with the same 5 to 10-degree drag travel angle.

- Cover the first fill pass by 1/2 to 2/3 and melt into the upper bevel. A slight "W" motion maybe needed to flatten & spread the bead.

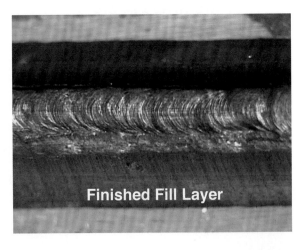

Finished Fill Layer

The finished layer should have:

- a flat to slightly convex contour that spreads evenly across the joint.
- complete fusion into both bevels
- joint filled out completely from one end of the workpiece to the other.

A common problem is insufficient fill at the upper bevel. If needed, add another fill pass to even out the weld and get a consistent weld with a smooth transition.

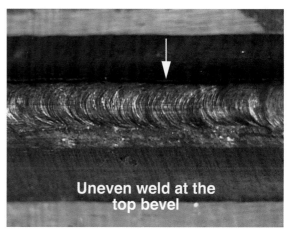

Uneven weld at the top bevel

5. Remaining Fill Layers

- Switch to 1/8 inch E7018 electrodes and increase the amperage.
- Allow the workpiece to cool briefly, or switch to another workpiece.
- Use the same 5 to 10-degrees work angle…with the same 5 to 10-degree drag travel angle.

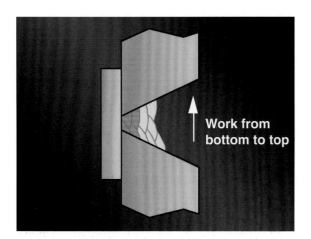

Work from bottom to top

In the horizontal position, always begin at the bottom of the joint and work upwards, allowing the previous bead to provide support for the next bead in the sequence.

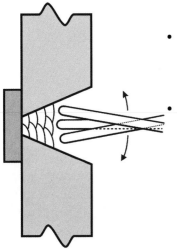

- You will need to vary work angles slightly for each bead in order to produce a layer with proper bead overlap.
- Make sure that each weld covers the previous bead by about one-half to two-thirds to produce a smooth contour.

- The finished layer should have a flat to slightly convex contour that spreads evenly across the joint with complete fusion into both bevels. The joint must be filled out from one end of the workpiece to the other.

Finished Second Fill Layer

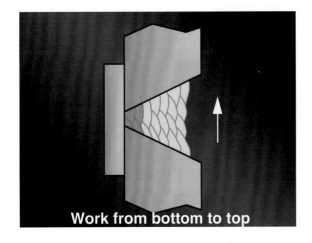

Work from bottom to top

- Use the same electrode angles and techniques for the remaining fill layers.
- Allow the workpiece to cool briefly in between layers, or switch to another workpiece.
- Start each layer at the bottom of the joint and work towards the top.
- If the layer is not even and smooth from bottom to top, add another fill pass to even out the layer.

6. Final Fill and Cover Layer

Final Fill Layer

- Allow the workpiece to cool briefly, or switch to another workpiece.
- Use the same 5 to 10-degrees work angle, with the same 5 to 10-degree drag travel angle.

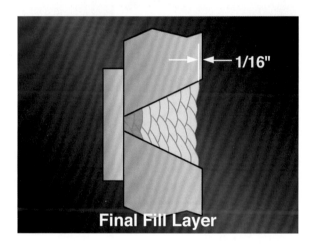

Final Fill Layer

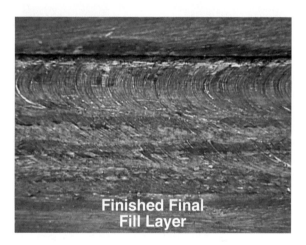

Finished Final Fill Layer

- Finished weld should be flat to slightly convex with complete fusion between the base metal and the weld metal and should fill the joint to within 1/16 inch to the top surface of the base metal.
- The weld should fill the joint from one end of the workpiece to the other.

If the distance is more than a 1/16 inch from the weld metal to the surface of the base metal, deposit additional fill passes as necessary, before depositing the cover layer.

Cover Layer

- Allow the workpiece to cool briefly, or switch to another workpiece.
- Use a drag travel angle of 5 to 10 degrees and a work angle of approximately 90 degrees.

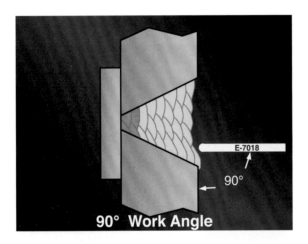

90° Work Angle

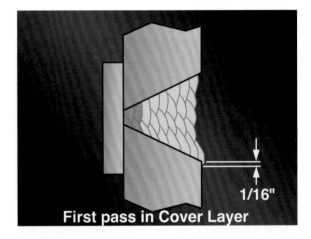

First pass in Cover Layer

- Melt into the bottom edge of the joint by a sixteenth of an inch to ensure complete fusion.
- Deposit the remaining beads using the same electrode angles
- Make sure that each weld covers the previous bead by about one-half to two-thirds to produce a smooth contour.

- The last pass in the cover layer should melt into the top edge of the joint by about a sixteenth of an inch.

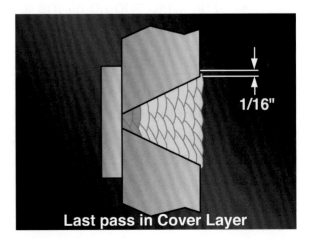

Last pass in Cover Layer

- The finished **Cover Layer** should have a smooth contour and shall be a minimum of flush with the base metal to a maximum of 1/8 inch reinforcement.

- There should be no edge weld undercut or weld bead overlap.

- The weld should have complete fusion into the sides of the joint and previously deposited weld metal.

- The joint must be filled out completely from one end of the workpiece to the other

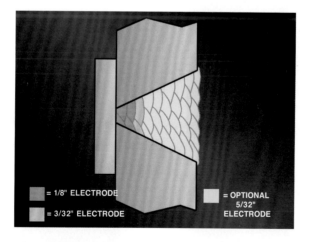

As your welding skill improves, you have the option of switching to 5/32 inch E7018 electrodes for the fourth and remaining layers. ...*Remember to increase the amperage.*

Inspect welds and continue practice

 EW369 SMAWA1

TOPIC 13

AIR CARBON ARC CUTTING AND GOUGING

Objective: **To show the equipment and method of operation required to use the air carbon arc cutting process.**

Introduction

The fabrication of metal products makes it necessary to cut parts to size or remove any unwanted material.

This can be done by either mechanical or thermal methods. Mechanical cutting methods such as sawing, shearing, blanking, milling, and grinding all require special machinery and fixtures, which sometimes limit their usefulness to welders.

Cutting with Band Saw

Thermal cutting however is done with most of the same equipment used for welding. Oxyacetylene cutting can be done using a special cutting torch in place of the welding torch.

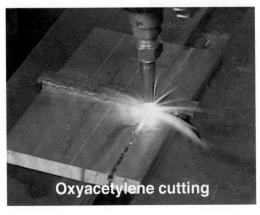
Oxyacetylene cutting

Thermal cutting has become a convenient and effective tool that welders can use for joint preparation, removal of bad welds and many other cutting and gouging operations.

Laser cutting and Water Jet cutting have also become more popular in automated applications of the fabrication industry.

Arc Cutting Processes

The four most commonly used arc cutting processes are:

- Carbon Arc
- Gas Tungsten Arc
- Shielded Metal Arc
- Plasma Arc

For this course, we will discuss Air Carbon Arc Cutting (CAC-A).

Air Carbon Arc

Air carbon arc cutting (CAC-A) is defined as an arc-cutting process where the severing of metals is caused by melting metal with the heat of an arc. An air stream is used to remove molten metal.

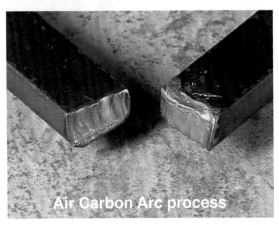
Air Carbon Arc process

The intense heat of the electric carbon arc melts the metal. A high-velocity jet of air blows the metal away before it can solidify as the arc moves on.

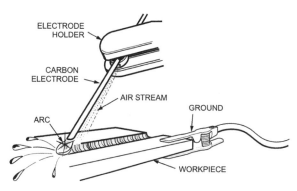

When cutting, the metal is cut completely through, while gouging melts partially through the metal, leaving a trough-like path where the molten metal has been removed.

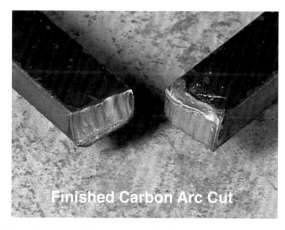
Finished Carbon Arc Cut

Gouging is used to remove defective welds, and to prepare grooves for welding.

Finished CAC-A Gouge

There is little tendency towards distortion and cracking, because the area of the cut is small, and the molten metal is quickly removed with minimum heat input.

The process is usually performed manually. However, a moving carriage may be used to convert it to an automatic operation. Air carbon arc cutting can be used in all positions; although the overhead position requires a high degree of skill.

Most common metals can be cut using CAC-A:

- carbon steel
- iron
- stainless steel
- most copper and nickel alloys
- magnesium and aluminum.

Before cutting or gouging stainless steel, aluminum, or other non-ferrous metals, a special cleaning process is required.

The process is **NOT** recommended for weld preparation of titanium, zirconium and similar metals without an additional cleaning procedure to remove surface material next to the cut.

If these metals are to be scrapped for re-melting, then this type of cutting is acceptable.

Equipment

Welding Unit

A conventional constant-current type power source is normally used.

Constant voltage type sources can be used, providing that extra care is taken to operate them within their rated output of current and duty cycle.

This is done by limiting the size of the electrode.

Alternating current power sources that have the conventional drooping characteristics can be used. Alternating current type electrodes must be used with these power sources.

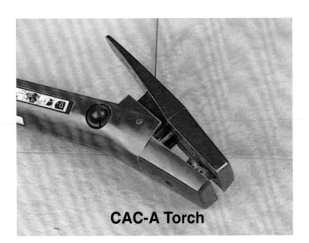

CAC-A Torch

Electrode Holder

The carbon arc holder contains a circular grip head that is grooved for holding the electrode, and is drilled to provide air jets.

The head can be rotated to allow various electrode angles.

The air jets are aligned with the groove so that the compressed air stream is always directed along the electrode on the side next to the material to be cut.

Close up of air jet holes

Air Supply

The airflow is controlled by a valve on the holder. The required air pressure ranges from 80 to 100 pounds per square inch.

Airflow can range from 5 cubic feet per minute to 50 cubic feet per minute.

Electrodes

Electrodes are a mixture of pure carbon, graphite, and a binder, baked to form a solid structure.

There are three types of electrodes: plain, carbon-graphite, and copper-coated.

The plain uncoated electrodes are less expensive, use less current, and start easier.

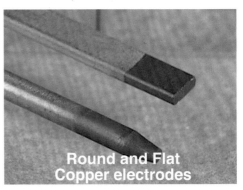

Round and Flat Copper electrodes

There are two electrode designs: the round type, and the flat type. Both are available with copper coating

Copper-coated electrodes provide better electrical conductivity between the electrode and the holder, are better for maintaining original diameter, last longer, and carry more current.

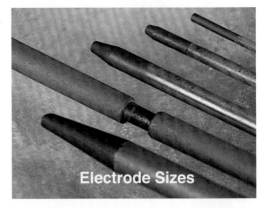

Electrode Sizes

Round electrodes are primarily used for gouging and cutting where flat electrodes are used for removal of excess surface metal.

The rounded electrodes are more common, and are normally operated with direct current, electrode positive.

Round electrodes range in diameter from 5/32 inch to 1 inch.

Electrodes are available in 6 inch and 12 inch lengths. For automatic operation, electrodes with tapered socket joints are available up to 17 inches in length.

Safety and Personal Protection Equipment (PPE)

In addition to the normal safety precautions for arc welding, there are a couple of extra safety precautions which must be observed with carbon arc (CAC-A) cutting and gouging.

A large volume of high velocity molten metal is displaced with Air carbon arc and requires extra care and protection. Be sure the molten metal is directed away from any equipment and personnel.

Also, a high noise level requires proper ear protection to be used with carbon arc. Always use OSHA approved earplugs and/or hearing protection.

Procedure

For cutting or gouging, **adjust the air pressure to about 80 to 100 psi** and then start the air flow from the arc torch by pressing the shutoff button.

Air flow shutoff button

The operator strikes an arc between the electrode and the work.

The electrode travel angle is approximately **35 to 45 degrees push** and the travel speed is relatively fast, depending on the depth of gouge needed. The greater the electrode angle, the deeper the gouge; lesser electrode angles cause a shallower gouge.

Air Carbon Arc Cutting

Summary

The air carbon arc cutting and gouging process has a wide variety of uses, such as back gouging of full penetration weld joints, preparing the joints for welding and removing defective weld metal.

You will find the air carbon arc process to be very useful for expanding your versatility as a welder.

Objective: To produce quality multi-pass single V-groove welds in the horizontal... or 2G position with a backing strip, that passes a visual inspection and a side bend test.

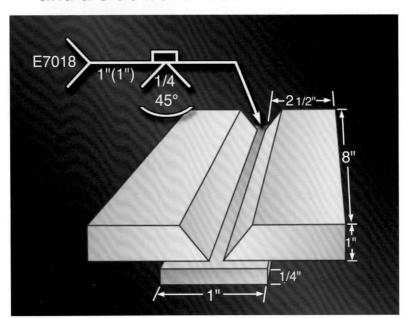

1. Materials & Machine Settings

Base Metal: 1" (25mm) x 2 1/2" (63.5mm) x 8" (203mm) mild steel plates
1/4" (6.35mm) x 1" (25mm) x 10" (254mm) mild steel backing strip

Electrodes: 3/32" E7018 (Root & First Fill Layer)
1/8" E7018 (Fill & Cover Layers)
5/32" E7018 (Optional Fill & Cover Layers)

Polarity: DCEP (Reverse Polarity)

Amperage: 80-100 (Root & First Fill Layer)
90-150 (Fill & Cover Layers)
110-230 (Optional Fill & Cover Layers)

2. Prepare Workpiece & Weld

Prepare a single V-groove weld in a butt joint using a set of test plates by following the instructions given in Topic 12.

3. Visual Inspection

Cracks

A weld shall be acceptable by visual inspection if it shows that the weld has no cracks; otherwise, it shall be considered as having failed.

Cracks

Fusion

A weld shall be acceptable by visual inspection if it shows that there is complete fusion between weld metal and base metal, as well as with previously deposited weld metal; otherwise, it shall be considered as having failed.

Incomplete Fusion

Slag Inclusions

A weld shall be acceptable by visual inspection if there is no slag inclusion that exceeds 1/8" in any 6 inches of weld; otherwise, it shall be considered as having failed.

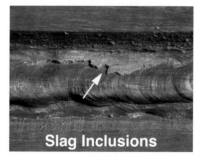
Slag Inclusions

Undercut

A weld shall be acceptable by visual inspection if undercut does not exceed 1/32" wide, 1/32" deep and has no more than the combined total of 2" of undercut in any 6 inches of weld.

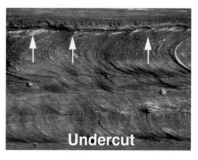
Undercut

Porosity

A weld shall be acceptable by visual inspection if porosity does not exceed 1/16" maximum and has no more than the combined total of 1/8" in any one square inch of weld; otherwise, it shall be considered as having failed.

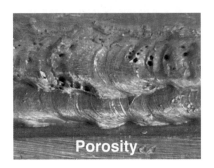

Porosity

Overlap

The weld shall be acceptable if there is no overlap. Overlap (cold lap) occurs when the weld metal rolls up on the base metal or previously deposited weld metal without fusion.

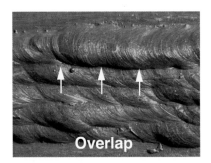

Overlap

Reinforcement

A weld shall be acceptable by visual inspection if the face reinforcement does not exceed the specified dimension and shows a gradual transition of the surface of the base metal. Any reinforcement must blend smoothly into the plate or previous weld surface with transition areas free from edge weld undercut.

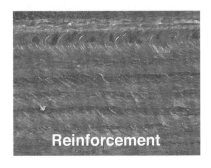

Reinforcement

1/8" Maximum Reinforcement

For this single V-groove weld the face reinforcement shall be a minimum of flush with the base metal, to a maximum of 1/8 inch, otherwise it shall be considered as having failed.

- Mark 2 test straps 3/8" wide about 1" on either side of the centerline.
- Stamp specimens with your identification.
- Cut straps and discard end pieces.

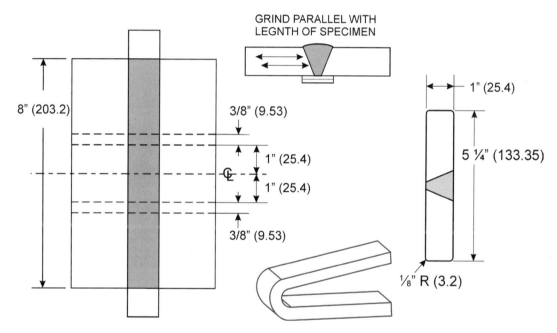

GRIND PARALLEL WITH
LEGNTH OF SPECIMEN

8" (203.2)

3/8" (9.53)

1" (25.4)

C_L

1" (25.4)

3/8" (9.53)

1" (25.4)

5 ¼" (133.35)

⅛" R (3.2)

- Reduce thickness of backing strip to about 1/8".
- Grind face and root side of each specimen flush to surface of base metal.
- Grind sides of specimens smooth.
- Grind 1/8" radius along each edge.
- Bend each specimen and examine the convex surfaces.

EW369 SMAWA1

Standards of Acceptability

The convex surface of the specimen shall contain no discontinuities exceeding the following dimensions:

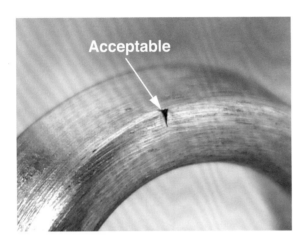

1/8" (3.2mm) measured in any direction on the surface.

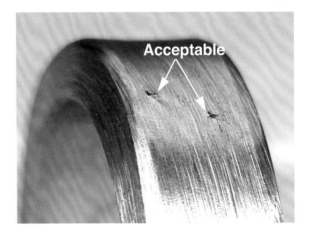

A sum of 3/8" (9.5mm) of the greatest dimensions of all discontinuities exceeding 1/32" but less than or equal to 1/8".

Analyze test results and check with your instructor.

SINGLE V-GROOVE WELD, BUTT JOINT, VERTICAL (3G) POSITION

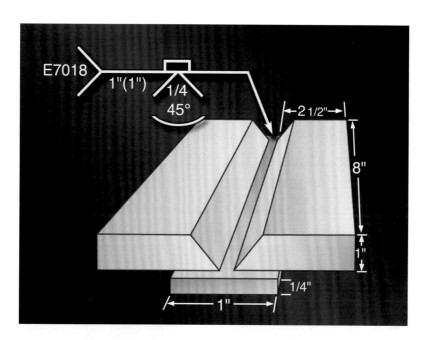

1. Materials & Machine Settings

Base Metal: 1" (25mm) x 2 1/2" (63.5mm) x 8" (203mm) mild steel plates
1/4" (6.35mm) x 1" (25mm) x 10" (254mm) mild steel backing strip

Electrodes: 3/32" E7018 (Root & First Fill Layer)
1/8" E7018 (Fill & Cover Layers)
5/32" E7018 (Optional Fill & Cover Layers)

Polarity: DCEP (Reverse Polarity)

Amperage: 80-100 (Root & First Fill Layer)
90-150 (Fill & Cover Layers)
110-230 (Optional Fill & Cover Layers)

2. Tack Weld & Position Workpiece

- Bevel two 1" plates with 22-1/2 degree angles and assemble a workpiece using the instructions given in Topic 12.

- Clamp in vertical (3G) position.

3. Deposit Root Pass

- Using a 3/32 inch E7018 electrode, center the electrode in the joint and strike the arc. Move up the joint with a slight Z-weave motion.

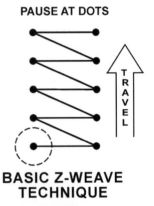

PAUSE AT DOTS

TRAVEL

BASIC Z-WEAVE TECHNIQUE

90° Work Angle

90° to 5° Push Travel Angle

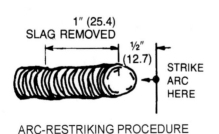

1" (25.4)
SLAG REMOVED
1/2" (12.7)
STRIKE ARC HERE

ARC-RESTRIKING PROCEDURE

- If a **restart** is necessary, clean the slag from crater thoroughly. Position the electrode about 1/2" in front of the crater. Strike the arc and move the electrode back, retrace the crater and resume normal travel.

- Finished weld should completely cover the backing strip and have complete fusion into both bevels. The joint must be filled out from one end of the workpiece to the other.

4. First Fill Layer

First Pass

- Same electrode and amp settings as root pass.
- Use a 10 to 15° work angle so that the electrode favors the bevel. Use the same 90° to 5° push travel angle
- Beginning at either toe, travel up joint using a slight side to side oscillation. Travel at a speed to produce a bead about 2 to 2-1/ 2" electrode diameters in width.

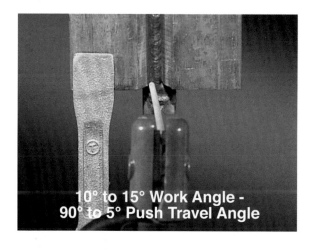

10° to 15° Work Angle -
90° to 5° Push Travel Angle

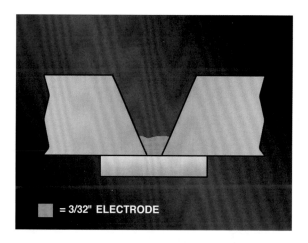

= 3/32" ELECTRODE

- Finished weld should melt into the bevel and cover the root pass by about one half to two-thirds and should have a flat to slightly convex contour.
- The joint must be filled out from one end of the workpiece to the other.

Second pass

- Use the same electrode and amp settings as the first fill pass.
- Use a 10 to 15° work angle so that the electrode favors the bevel. Use the same 90° to 5° push travel angle.

90° to 5° Push Travel Angle

- Starting at the opposite toe, travel up joint using a slight side to side oscillation. Produce a bead that melts into the bevel and covers the first fill pass by about a half.

- The finished layer should have a flat to slightly convex contour that spreads evenly across the joint and is fused into both bevels.

- The joint should also be completely filled from one end of the workpiece to the other.

- Switch to a 1/8th inch E7018 electrode and increase the amperage.

- Allow the workpiece to cool briefly, or switch to another workpiece.

- Beginning at either toe, use the same 10 to 15° work angle and the same 90° to 5° push travel angle, deposit the remaining fill layers.

- You may need to adjust the work angle slightly in order to get a layer with proper bead overlap.

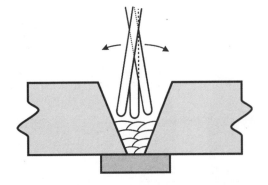

- The Finished layer should be flat to slightly convex and distributed evenly across the joint

- The layer should have complete fusion into both bevels and between the base metal and the weld metal.

- The joint should also be completely filled from one end of the workpiece to the other.

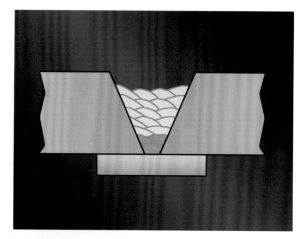

Completed Fill Layer

6. Final Fill and Cover Layer

Final Fill Layer

- Use the same electrode angles and techniques for the remaining fill layer.
- Use the same 90° work angle and the same 90° to 5° push travel angle
- Finished weld should be flat to slightly convex with complete fusion between the base metal and the weld metal and should fill the joint to within 1/16 inch to the top surface of the base metal.

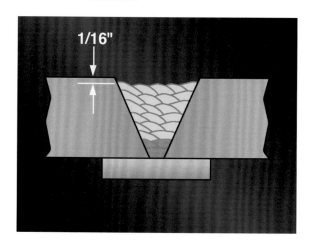

1/16"

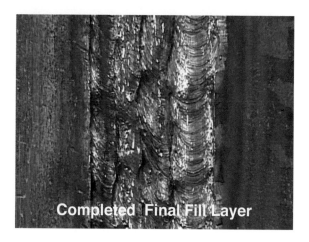

Completed Final Fill Layer

If the distance is more than a 1/16 inch deposit additional fill passes as necessary, before depositing the cover layer.

Cover Layer

- Allow the workpiece to cool briefly, or switch to another workpiece.

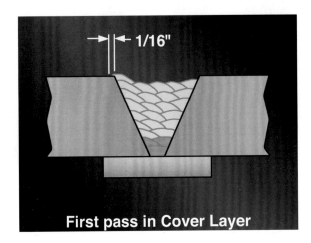

First pass in Cover Layer

- Use a push travel angle of 90 to 5 degrees and a work angle of approximately 90 degrees.
- The first bead of the cover pass should melt into the edge of the joint by about 1/16 inch to insure complete fusion.
- Deposit the remaining beads in the cover layer making sure that each bead covers the previous bead by about one half to two-thirds to produce a smooth contour.

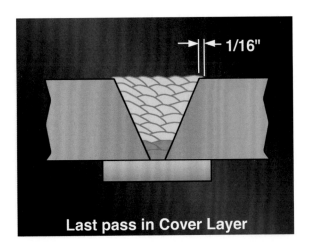

Last pass in Cover Layer

Finished Weld

- The last bead of the cover layer should melt into the edge of the joint by about 1/16 inch to insure complete fusion.

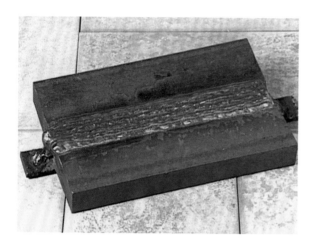

- The finished **Cover Layer** should have a smooth contour and shall be a minimum of flush with the base metal to a maximum of 1/8 inch reinforcement.
- There should be no edge weld undercut or weld bead overlap.

- The weld should have complete fusion into the sides of the joint and previously deposited weld metal.
- The joint must be filled out completely from one end of the workpiece to the other

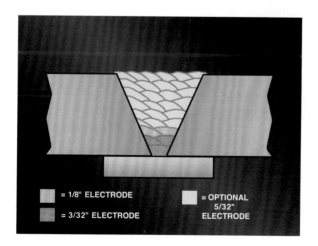

= 1/8" ELECTRODE

= 3/32" ELECTRODE

= OPTIONAL 5/32" ELECTRODE

As your welding skill improves, you have the option of switching to 5/32 inch E7018 electrodes for the fourth and remaining layers. ...*Remember to increase the amperage.*

Inspect welds and continue practice

EW369 SMAWA1

METALS IDENTIFICATION
FOR WELDING

Objective: **To help you identify metals based on several methods of testing.**

In order to make a good weld, it is necessary to know the type and composition of the base metal. Under production conditions, it is easy as the metal is color coded.

But there will be times when you must figure out for yourself what the metal is and you must know enough about the composition of the metal to set up the required welding procedure.

Most of the more common metals, such as cast iron, stainless steel, steel, aluminum alloy, and magnesium are quite easy to identify.

However, less common metals such as titanium, zirconium, tungsten, and other special alloys, are more difficult to identify.

Here are a few methods you can use to help identify the various types of metal.

Metal Identification Process

Shape or Use of a part

The **shape or use** of a part is a clue to the type of metal it is made of.

A piece of strap iron... is probably low carbon steel.

And a piece of angle iron is probably low carbon steel.

A lifting hook will likely be heat-treated alloy steel.

Links of a roller chain are probably high carbon alloy, also heat-treated.

Magnetic Attraction

Magnetic attraction, appearance, and **weight,** can also be used to identify metal.

Some metals... like mild steel are strongly magnetic, some, like Incoloy®... a little magnetic, and some... like aluminum... are non-magnetic.

Non-Magnetic Group

Metals in the non-magnetic group are:

- Aluminum alloy
- magnesium
- lead
- copper
- stainless steel (although some are magnetic)
- and alloys of copper (brass, Bronze)

There are also less common metals such as :

- titanium
- zirconium
- tantalum
- and tungsten

This group of metals requires different welding procedures than those used on low carbon steels.

We can recognize aluminum alloy by its silvery appearance. It is also lighter and softer than steel.

Magnesium is a little, lighter in weight than aluminum; the cut surface appears dull grey with a slight brownish tone. If struck, it has a dull ring as compared to the bell-like ring for steel or aluminum.

Stainless Steel

These heavy non-magnetic pieces are stainless steel. Stainless is a little unusual because some types are magnetic. It usually shows no sign of rust or corrosion.

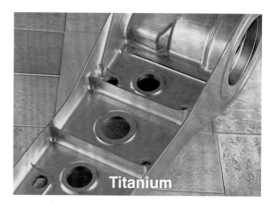

Titanium

Titanium, which is lighter and stronger than aluminum or magnesium. It's often used in aircraft and rockets where lightweight components with high strength are required.

It's also used for highly priced golf clubs and bicycle frames.

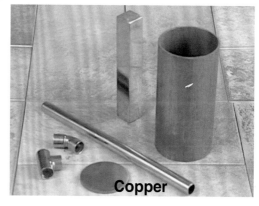

Copper

Copper, the color of a penny is easy to recognize. Alloys of copper, such as brass, are more yellowish in appearance.

Lead is much heavier than steel or brass and is very soft.

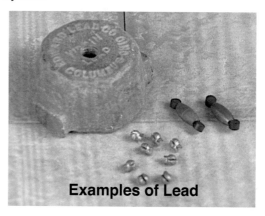

Examples of Lead

The other metals in this non-magnetic group... zirconium, tantalum, and tungsten... can be identified by checking a number of different characteristics.

You'll become familiar with these characteristics as your experience increases.

Slightly Magnetic Group

This slightly magnetic piece is commonly known as Incoloy®... an alloy of nickel, copper, and iron; in some alloys it is non-magnetic.

Incoloy®

To weld Incoloy® requires special electrodes and procedures.

Magnetic Group

We can identify cast iron quite easily because it LOOKS like a casting.

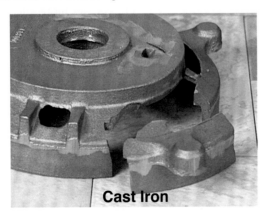

Cast Iron

Cast iron is brittle. If it is broken, the surface appears dark grey and there will be little or no sign of bending.

Galvanized Steel

Galvanized steel has a silvery-grey zinc coating that must be removed before welding.

Chisel Test, Grinding and Cutting

By chiseling a small notch into a metal sample, or grinding metal, you can also determine type and composition.

A chiseled notch in cast iron looks different than steel...

and a notch in steel...

looks different than aluminum.

A **spark test** can also be used to determine types of steel. Each type of steel gives off a different spark when ground with a fast-turning emery wheel.

Welding textbooks illustrate and describe how sparks from each steel-composition looks.

Material	Test					
	Appearance Test	Magnetic Test	Chisel Test	Fracture Test	Flame Test	Spark Test*
Low Carbon Steel	Dark Grey	Strongly Magnetic	Continuous Chip Smooth Edges Chips Easily	Bright Grey	Melts Fast Becomes Bright Red Before Melting	Long Yellow Carrier Lines (Approx. 20% Carbon or Below)
Medium Carbon Steel	Dark Grey	Strongly Magnetic	Continuous Chip Smooth Edges Chips Easily	Very Light Grey	Melts Fast Becomes Bright Red Before Melting	Yellow Line Sprigs Very Plain Now (Approx. 20% to 45% Carbon)
High Carbon Steel	Dark Grey	Strongly Magnetic	Hard to Chip Can be Continuous	Very Light Grey	Melts Fast Becomes Bright Red Before Melting	Yellow Line Bright Burst Very Clean Many Star Bursts (Approx. 45% Carbon and Above)
High Sulfur Steel	Dark Grey	Strongly Magnetic	Continuous Chip Smooth Edges Chips Easily	Bright Grey Fine Grain	Melts Fast Becomes Bright Red Before Melting	Swelling Carrier Lines, Cigar Shape
Manganese Steel	Dull Cast Surface	Non-Magnetic	Extremely Hard to Chisel	Course Grained	Melts Fast Becomes Bright Red Before Melting	Bright White, Fan-Shaped Burst
Stainless Steel	Bright, Silvery Smooth	Depends on Exact Analysis	Continuous Chip Smooth Bright Color	Depends on Type Bright	Melts Fast Becomes Bright Red Before Melting	1. Nickel - Black Shape Close to Wheel 2. Moly - Short Arrow Shape Tongue (only) 3. Vanadium - Long Spearpoint Tongue (only)
Cast Iron	Dull Grey, Evidence of Sand Mold	Strongly Magnetic	Small Chips About 1/8 in. Not Easy to Chip, Brittle	Brittle	Melts Fast Becomes Dull Red Before Melting	Red Carrier Lines (Very Little Carbon Exists)
Wrought Iron	Light Grey, Smooth	Strongly Magnetic	Continuous Chip Smooth Edges Chips Easily	Bright Grey Fibrous Appearance	Melts Fast Becomes Bright Red Before Melting	Long, Straw Color Lines (Practially Free of Bursts or Sprigs)

*For best results, use at least 5000 surface feet per minute on grinding equipment.
(Cir. X R.P.M.)/12 = S.F. per Min.

EW369 SMAWA1

Remember that the electrode composition must be matched to the composition of the metal.

If you collect a number of sample pieces of known composition, you can use them to make a direct comparison to the sparking of the unknown metal.

As your ability to weld various kinds and types of metal grows, so should your ability to identify them.

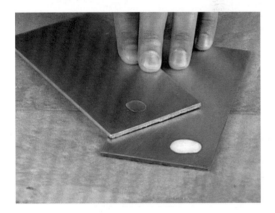

Finally... you should know that chemical and other tests are available for metal identification.

After you have identified a specific type of metal... you are ready to use your welding skills.

Objective: To produce a quality multi-pass single V-groove weld in the overhead or 4G position with a backing strip, that passes a visual inspection and side bend test.

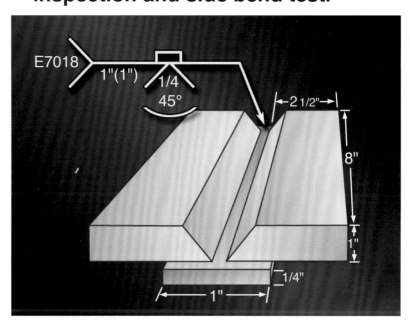

1. Materials & Machine Settings

Base Metal: 1" (25mm) x 2 1/2" (63.5mm) x 8" (203mm) mild steel plates
1/4" (6.35mm) x 1" (25mm) x 10" (254mm) mild steel backing strip

Electrodes: 3/32" E7018 (Root & First Fill Layer)
1/8" E7018 (Fill & Cover Layers)
5/32" E7018 (Optional Fill & Cover Layers)

Polarity: DCEP (Reverse Polarity)

Amperage: 80-100 (Root & First Fill Layer)
90-150 (Fill & Cover Layers)
110-230 (Optional Fill & Cover Layers)

2. Tack Weld & Position Workpiece

- Bevel two 1" plates with 22-1/2 degree angles and assemble a workpiece using the instructions given in Topic 12.
- Clamp in the overhead (4G) position.

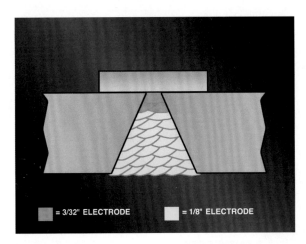

= 3/32" ELECTRODE   = 1/8" ELECTRODE

- This weld involves 9 layers. Deposit the root and first fill layer with 3/32" electrodes and the remaining fill and cover layers with 1/8 inch electrodes. The actual bead count may vary depending on weld size, bead placement and other factors such as root opening and bevel angle.

3. Deposit Root Pass

- Center the electrode in the joint and strike the arc. Move down the joint with a slight Z-weave motion.

90° Work Angle

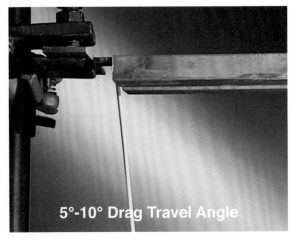

5°-10° Drag Travel Angle

- If a **restart** is necessary, clean the slag from crater thoroughly. Position the electrode about 1/2" in front of the crater. Strike the arc and move the electrode back, retrace the crater and resume normal travel.

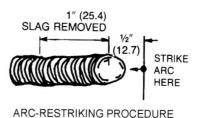

1" (25.4)
SLAG REMOVED
½" (12.7)
STRIKE ARC HERE

ARC-RESTRIKING PROCEDURE

- Finished weld should completely cover the backing strip and have complete fusion into both bevels. The joint must be filled out from one end of the workpiece to the other.

4. First Fill Layer

First Pass

- Same electrode and amp settings as root pass.
- Use a 10 to 15° work angle so that the electrode favors the bevel. Use the same 5° to 10° drag travel angle.
- Beginning at either toe, travel along the joint using a slight side to side oscillation. Travel at a speed to produce a bead about 2 to 2-1/2 electrode diameters in width.

5°-10°
Work Angle

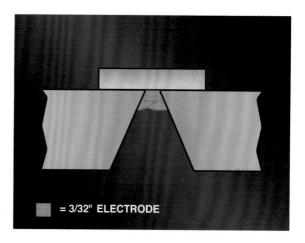

= 3/32" ELECTRODE

- The weld should melt into the bevel and cover the root pass by about one-half to two-thirds and should have a flat to slightly convex contour.

Second pass

- Use the same electrode and amp settings as the first fill pass.

- Use a 10 to 15° work angle so that the electrode favors the bevel. Use the same 5° to 10° drag travel angle.

- Starting at the opposite toe, travel down the joint using the same technique as the first pass. Produce a bead that melts into the bevel and covers the first fill pass by about a half.

- The finished layer should have a flat to slightly convex contour that spreads evenly across the joint and is fused into both bevels.

- The joint should also be completely filled from one end of the workpiece to the other.

5. Remaining Fill Layers

- Switch to a 1/8 inch E7018 electrode and increase the amperage.

- Allow the workpiece to cool briefly, or switch to another workpiece.

- Using the same 5° to 10° drag travel angle, deposit the remaining fill layers.

- You will need to adjust the work angle slightly in order to get a layer with proper bead overlap.

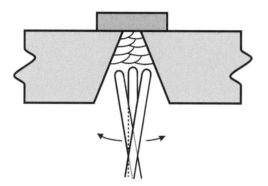

- The finished layer should have a flat to slightly convex contour that spreads evenly across the joint.

- The layer should have complete fusion into both bevels and between the base metal and the weld metal.

- The joint should also be completely filled from one end of the workpiece to the other.

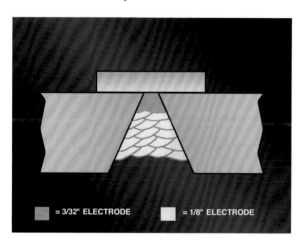

= 3/32" ELECTRODE   = 1/8" ELECTRODE

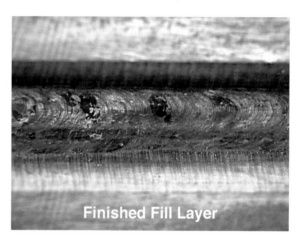

Finished Fill Layer

6. Final Fill and Cover Layer

Final Fill Layer

- Use the same work angle and the same 5° to 10° drag travel angle.

- The finished layer should be flat to slightly convex and distributed evenly across the joint with complete fusion into both bevels.

- The layer should be filled out completely, from one end of the workpiece to the other and should fill the joint to within a sixteenth of an inch from the surface of the base metal.

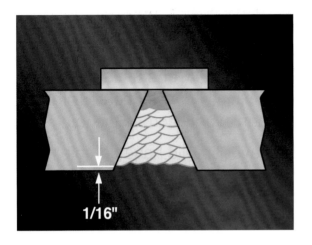

Completed Final Fill Layer

If the distance is more than a 1/16 inch deposit additional fill passes as necessary, before depositing the cover layer.

Cover Layer

- Allow the workpiece to cool breifly, or switch to another workpiece.

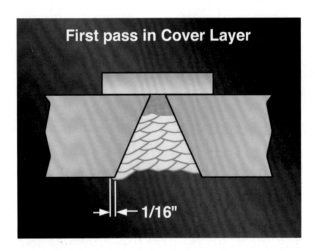

First pass in Cover Layer

1/16"

- Use a 90° work angle and 5° to 10° drag travel angle to deposit the cover pass.
- The first bead of the cover pass should melt into the edge of the joint by about 1/16 inch to insure complete fusion.
- Deposit the remaining beads in the cover layer making sure that each bead covers the previous bead by about one half to two-thirds to produce a smooth contour.

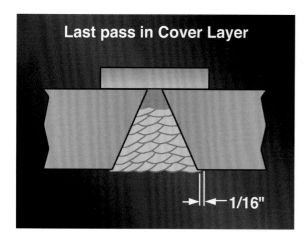

Last pass in Cover Layer

1/16"

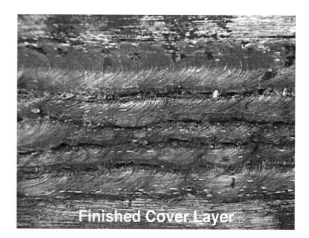

Finished Cover Layer

- The last bead of the cover layer should melt into the edge of the joint by about 1/16 inch to insure complete fusion.
- The finished **Cover Layer** should have a smooth contour and shall be a minimum of flush with the base metal to a maximum of 1/8 inch reinforcement.
- There should be no edge weld undercut or weld bead overlap.

- The weld should have complete fusion into the sides of the joint and previously deposited weld metal.
- The joint must be filled out completely from one end of the workpiece to the other

 EW369 SMAWA1

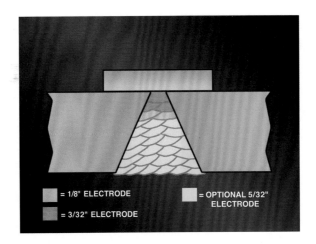

= 1/8" ELECTRODE
= 3/32" ELECTRODE
= OPTIONAL 5/32" ELECTRODE

As your welding skill improves, you have the option of switching to 5/32 inch E7018 electrodes for the fourth and remaining layers. ...*Remember to increase the amperage.*

Inspect welds and continue practice

WELDING CAST IRON AND HARD SURFACING WELDS

Objective: To learn the factors that must be considered in welding cast iron and the steps that must be taken to apply surfacing welds to machinery to improve wear or for restoration.

Introduction

There are several types of cast iron. However, grey iron is more widely used than any other type.

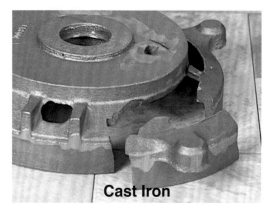
Cast Iron

Iron castings have a tough skin, which may have flaws such as air holes and mixed-in foundry sand.

It is brittle: it will break, rather than bend, when hit with a hard blow.

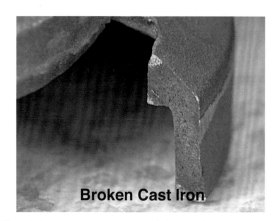
Broken Cast Iron

The dark grey appearance of the broken surface is due to the free carbon, and is the reason it is called grey iron.

Cast iron is difficult to weld because the heat of welding can cause some of the free carbon to combine with other elements, and make the casting more brittle.

Welding is done on cast iron in the manufacture of new parts, repair of faulty new castings, and repair of castings that have been broken during use.

Welding Cast Iron

General Conditions

When possible, get information from the manufacturer of the casting, regarding welding procedures.

> Although each welding job will likely be different from the last, there are several procedures that must be considered on ALL jobs.

Joint preparation for cast iron is similar to that used for steel. The joint may be formed by chipping, chiseling, or grinding.

V-grooves should be somewhat wider; about 75 to 90 degree included angles.

The skin must be ground back from the edge of the groove, and from the root side, if welding is to be done there too.

Joint preparation

The weld area must be clean, and free from oil, paint, and other contaminants.

> *You should weld the part while it's hot. Preheat the entire part to 600 degrees Fahrenheit. Small parts, up to about 30 pounds, can be heated with a torch or in a furnace.*

When filling a joint in cast iron, it's sometimes necessary to first coat, or butter, the entire surface of the joint with light-penetration string beads.

"Buttered" joint

If buttering is not necessary... deposit a root bead... then finish filling the joint as needed. Allow the finished weld to cool slowly.

Electrodes for Cast Iron

Four of the types of electrodes available for arc-welding cast iron are:

- Cast iron
- Copper-base alloy
- Nickel-base alloy
- Mild steel.

Today, nickel and nickel-based alloy electrodes are most commonly used for welding cast iron. Their selection depends on the:

- Machinability of the weld
- Color-match of the weld to the base metal
- The strength of the weld
- The ductility of the weld.

NICKEL ELECTRODES contain mostly nickel, with small amounts of iron, carbon and copper. These are often referred to as **"straight"** nickel electrodes.

They produce welds similar to the nickel-based alloy electrodes, but are usually used in low stress welds on light or medium weight castings, where good machinability is desired.

They do not provide a good color match.

Electrodes for Cast Iron

NICKEL-BASED ALLOY ELECTRODES contain about 55% nickel and a trace of carbon. The remainder of the electrode is iron.

These produce a stronger, more ductile weld with good machinability. Although they do not provide a good color match these welds have a much better resistance to hot-cracking and have a lower coefficient of thermal expansion.

MILD STEEL ELECTRODES, classified as EST, are used only when machining is not required. The weld metal picks up carbon from the cast iron and becomes too hard to machine.

Typical Welding Procedure

A common type of weld you may be asked to do is on a cracked engine block.

In this case, a part of the casting is not broken off, but it is cracked through and allows water or oil to leak out.

Crack in Engine Block

Begin by drilling a pilot hole about one 1/8 inch diameter through the casting, at each end of the crack.

Then countersink the holes with a 1/4 inch bit. This will keep the crack from enlarging.

Prepared V-Groove joint

Chip or grind a vee groove between the chamfered holes, leaving about one-sixteenth inch of metal at the bottom of the groove. Remove the casting skin next to the groove and make sure the surface is free of oil and grease. Then weld with a high-nickel electrode laying down short beads.

To help relieve stress... peen the welds while they are still hot.

Finished Cast Iron Weld

The finished weld should have a smooth and even appearance.

Although each job may be different from the last one, here is a review of the things you should do EACH time you weld Cast Iron:

1. Make sure the metal is **clean**. A good weld cannot be made on a dirty joint.

2. Preheat the entire part if possible. **Weld while hot---cool slowly**. This will help keep the metal from becoming brittle at the weld.

3. Select the **proper electrode**.

4. Perhaps most importantly, when welding parts that are not preheated, be patient; **don't overheat**; weld a little at a time.

5. **Peen** the weld beads while still hot.

With study, practice, and experience, you will be able to make satisfactory welds on cast iron.

Hard Surface Welding

General Information

Surfacing is a welding process for coating steel with an alloy that resists wear or corrosion. It also includes building-up of surfaces that have been worn, to increase their life.

Surfacing is often applied to new parts as well, for the same reason.

The electrodes used for surfacing produce a very hard material that will withstand various types of wear. They can usually be applied only **1 to 3 layers thick**.

There are five major types of wear:

1. Abrasive (Scratching, Grinding and Gouging)

2. Impact

3. Adhesive

4. High Temperature

5. Corrosive

Manufacturers of surfacing electrodes provide excellent information to assist in selection and use of the correct material or combination of materials.

Hard Surfacing Electrodes

Layering

Electrodes are available in a range that varies from tough to hard.

Tough Material Applications

A typical example of surfacing, is on a bucket or dipper of a back-hoe. The wearing surface of this item is subject to heavy blows as well as abrasion.

Back-Hoe Bucket

Let us assume that we have found that the bucket material is manganese steel...

The recommended buildup material would therefore be selected from the **tough range**.

Work hardening means that as the surface of metals is hit or peened, it becomes harder in the area that it's hit.

Each time the surface is hit by a rock, it becomes harder at that point. Finally the entire surface becomes quite hard; the tough material underneath supports the surface and absorbs the heavy blows.

One or two layers of surfacing will produce a very hard surface that will increase the life several times.

A **single layer** of the hard material is somewhat mixed in with the base metal which reduces the possible hardness.

A **second layer** is used when maximum hardness is needed...and a **third layer** may be used with some materials.

There is a tendency for cracking and flaking off in use, but the small cracks that appear in some surfacing usually cause no trouble because they are only in the surface material.

The major difference between Hard Surfacing and Shielded Metal Arc Welding is that weld penetration is not desirable.

A good surfacing weld should have complete fusion with as little penetration into the base metal as possible.

Hard Surface Welding is an important process to learn. It can produce large dollar savings in several types of industry.

SINGLE V-GROOVE WELD, BUTT JOINT, FLAT (1G) POSITION

Objective: To produce a quality multi-pass single V-groove weld in the flat... or 1G position with a backing strip, that passes a visual inspection and a side bend test.

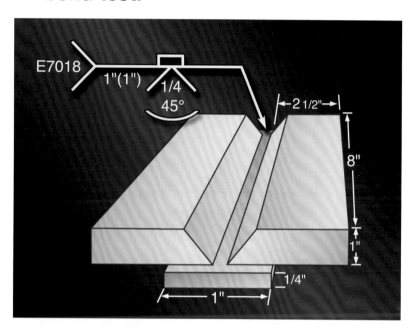

1. Materials & Machine Settings

Base Metal: 1" (25mm) x 2 1/2" (63.5mm) x 8" (203mm) mild steel plates
1/4" (6.35mm) x 1" (25mm) x 10" (254mm) mild steel backing strip

Electrodes: 1/8" E7018 (Root & First Fill Layer)
5/32" E7018 (Fill & Cover Layers)

Polarity: DCEP (Reverse Polarity)

Amperage: 90-150 (Root & First Fill Layer)
110-230 (Fill & Cover Layers)

NOTE: *Some machines run hotter than others. Lower amperage may make the puddle easier to control.*

2. Tack Weld & Position Workpiece

- Bevel two 1" plates with 22-1/2 degree angles and assemble a workpiece using the instructions given in Topic 12.

- Clamp in flat or (1G) position, or place the workpiece flat on the weld table.

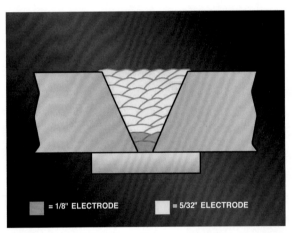

= 1/8" ELECTRODE   = 5/32" ELECTRODE

- This weld involves 9 layers. Deposit the root and first fill layer with 1/8 inch electrodes and the remaining fill and cover layers with 5/32" electrodes. The actual bead count may vary depending on weld size, bead placement and other factors such as root opening and bevel angle.

3. Deposit Root Pass

- Strike the arc and move smoothly along the joint with a slight side-to-side motion.

90° Work Angle

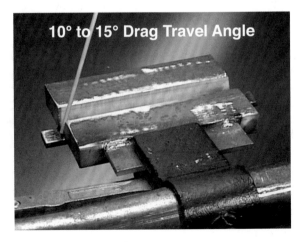

10° to 15° Drag Travel Angle

- If a **restart** is necessary, clean the slag from crater thoroughly.

  Position the electrode about 1/2" in front of the crater. Strike the arc and move the electrode back, retrace the crater and resume normal travel.

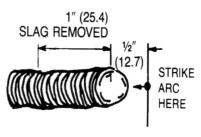

1" (25.4)
SLAG REMOVED
½" (12.7)
STRIKE ARC HERE

ARC-RESTRIKING PROCEDURE

- Finished weld should be flat to slightly convex, and have complete fusion into both bevels. The joint must be filled out from one end of the workpiece to the other.

4.   First Fill Layer

First Pass

- Same electrode and amp settings as root pass.
- Use a 10 to 15° work angle, so that the electrode favors the bevel. Use the same 10 to 15° drag travel angle.
- Focus on what is happening with the puddle. Travel along the joint with a steady drag. Travel at a speed to produce a consistent bead about 2 to 2-1/2 electrode diameters in width.

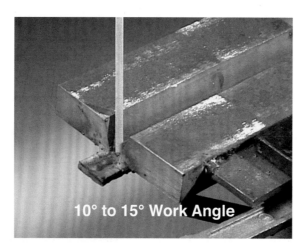

10° to 15° Work Angle

- Finished weld should melt into the bevel and cover the root pass by about one half and should have a flat to slightly convex contour.

Second pass

- Use the same electrode and amp settings as the first fill pass.
- Use a 10° to 15° work angle so that the electrode favors the bevel. Use the same 5° to 10° drag travel angle.
- Starting at the opposite toe, travel across the joint using the same technique as the first pass. The bead should melt into the bevel and cover the first fill pass by about a half to two thirds.

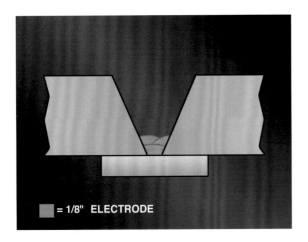

= 1/8" ELECTRODE

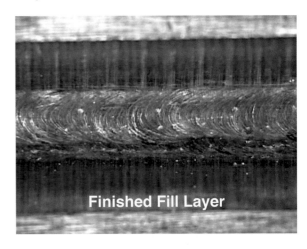

Finished Fill Layer

- The finished layer should have a flat to slightly convex contour that spreads evenly across the joint and is fused into both bevels.
- The joint should also be completely filled from one end of the workpiece to the other.

5. Remaining Fill Layers

- Switch to a 5/32 inch E7018 electrode and increase the amperage.
- Allow the workpiece to cool briefly, or switch to another workpiece.
- Using the same 5° to 10° drag travel angle, deposit the remaining fill layers.

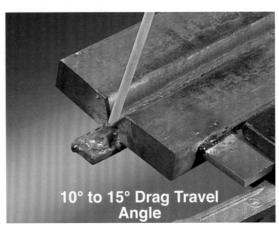

10° to 15° Drag Travel Angle

- You will need to adjust the work angle slightly in order to get a layer with proper bead overlap.

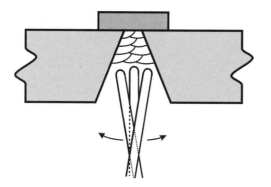

- The finished layer should have a flat to slightly convex contour that spreads evenly across the joint.

- The layer should have complete fusion into both bevels and between the base metal and the weld metal.

- The joint should also be completely filled from one end of the workpiece to the other.

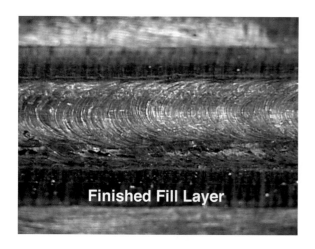

Finished Fill Layer

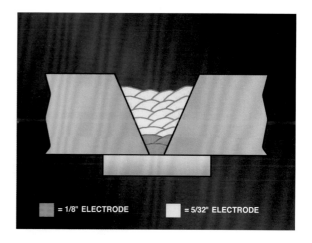

☐ = 1/8" ELECTRODE   ☐ = 5/32" ELECTRODE

6. Final Fill and Cover Layer

Final Fill Layer

- Use the same work angle and the same 5° to 10° drag travel angle.
- The finished layer should be flat to slightly convex with an even ripple pattern and should be distributed evenly across the joint with complete fusion into both bevels.
- The layer should be filled out completely, from one end of the workpiece to the other... and should fill the joint to within a sixteenth of an inch from the surface of the base metal.

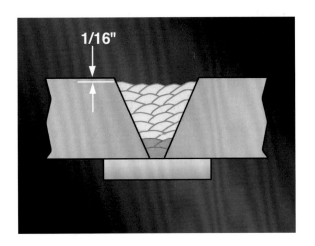

1/16"

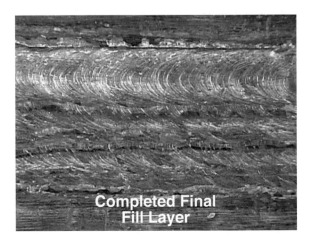

Completed Final Fill Layer

If the distance is more than a 1/16 inch, deposit additional fill passes as necessary before depositing the cover layer.

Cover Layer

- Allow the workpiece to cool breifly, or switch to another workpiece.

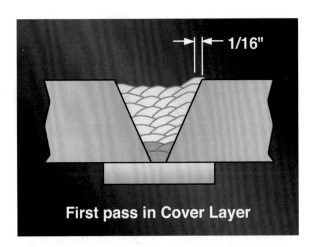

1/16"

First pass in Cover Layer

- Use a 90° work angle and 5° to 10° drag travel angle to deposit the cover pass.
- The first bead of the cover pass should melt into the edge of the joint by about 1/16 inch to insure complete fusion.
- Deposit the remaining beads in the cover layer making sure that each bead covers the previous bead by about one half to two-thirds to produce a smooth contour.

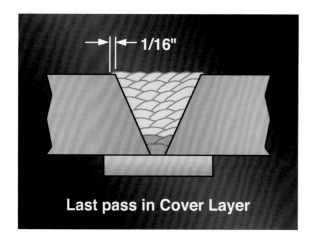

1/16"

Last pass in Cover Layer

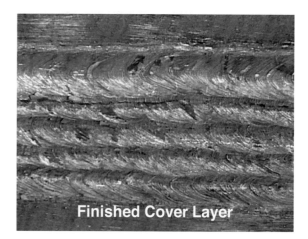

Finished Cover Layer

- The last bead of the cover layer should melt into the edge of the joint by about 1/16 inch to insure complete fusion.

- The finished **cover layer** should have a smooth contour and shall be a minimum of flush with the base metal to a maximum of 1/8 inch reinforcement.

- There should be no edge weld undercut or weld bead overlap.

- The weld should have complete fusion into the   sides of the joint and previously deposited weld metal.

- The joint must be filled out completely from one end of the workpiece to the other.

Inspect welds and continue practice

NOTES

EW369 SMAWA1